Wm.

THE HUMAN PROBLEMS
OF THE MINISTER

THE
HUMAN PROBLEMS
OF THE
MINISTER

❖ ❖ ❖

BY DANIEL D. WALKER

HARPER & BROTHERS · NEW YORK

Library of Congress catalog card number: 60-8134

For Virginia

CONTENTS

FOREWORD

❖ ❖ ❖

I remember a man, in my first church after seminary, who took delight in telling me how hard he worked. The implication was that I had an easy job compared with his. All I knew was that a day beginning at 5:30 A.M. and ending at 10 P.M. made me tired. The ministry is a hard job, and no man who expects to be less than the hardest-working man in his community ought to undertake it. This means, of course, that the minister must learn to deal with the innumerable tensions that are a part of his profession.

Not the least part of our difficulty is an unwillingness or an inability to face the tensions honestly and recognize our temptations in their subtle disguises. Certainly the beginning has to be a realistic analysis of what is involved. I speak with some insistence on this point, because I deal constantly with preachers who have never faced themselves or their problems. What an unusual thing it is to hear a man say, "I was at fault." Many a man could enter into a far greater ministry than he has ever known if he would crack the veneer of his pretense.

Now sometimes a minister will need professional help in getting a true appraisal of his trouble and his need. Yet he ever runs the risk of receiving a treatment that does as much harm as good. Usually, another minister will be his best help, for there is no healing for us unless the physician knows the job as well as the man.

All of this leads me to say that Daniel Walker's book is designed to help us recognize our ailments and that it points the way toward their elimination or control. He has been my friend for many years, and his ministry has reflected the wonderful quality of his own inner life. He has faced the tensions thoughtfully and practically. Every minister will find insights which will help him and will be stimulated to think through his own paradoxes. This is what I call a "starter" book because it prods a man to begin his own self-examination.

It is a fine privilege to introduce *The Human Problems of the Minister* to my brethren in the greatest fraternity in the world. I have hoped for a long time that something would come from the pen of this gifted preacher and pastor. He will do us all good.

Bishop Gerald Kennedy

HOLLYWOOD, CALIFORNIA

PREFACE

❖ ❖ ❖

The ideas expressed in this book are based on the simple conviction that although no man can serve two masters, most of us try. Spiritually oriented, we covet material rewards; apostles of the humble spirit, we give honors to others and seek them for ourselves; believing in love, we have been known to hate. Sometimes we suspect it is not two masters we serve, but two hundred and two.

In his second letter to the Corinthians, Paul writes, "We are handicapped on all sides but we are never frustrated" (Phillips). We will have to let Paul speak for himself in this, but as for the rest of us, freedom from frustration is not one of our most conspicuous achievements. We are living in highly complicated and confusing times in which pressures are intense.

It is with human tensions, as they appear in the clergy, that this material deals.

This book is not the result of a scientific study. I have made no surveys and have administered no psychological tests. My preparation for this writing is to have served twenty years in the ministry, experiencing its tensions first hand. At first I thought my reactions were unique. Gradually, however, I came to realize that many ministers, perhaps most of them, felt much the same as I, but were suppressing their feelings. It would seem to be a therapeutic experience for all of us to talk more freely about the tensions of our calling.

The last thing I want to do is to pose as an expert on ministerial problems. I have not shied away from proposing solutions when I have some to suggest, but I have not thought of myself in any sense as an authority. Rather, I am one of several thousand confused ministers across the country, and am merely trying to give expression to the problems that trouble all of us.

The basic question that runs throughout the book is, "What is the role of the minister in our generation?" It is a changing role. We no longer fit the pattern of the clergy of a hundred years ago, or even ten years ago. As we confront the tensions brought about by changing times, we are better prepared to reshape the ministry into a more effective instrument for God in our day. This book tries to show us how to face up to the tensions. It is left largely to the reader to reshape his own ministry—or, if he is a layman, to assist his minister in doing so.

My indebtedness to those who helped make the book possible is very great. It was the Reverend Myron Herrell who first suggested that I prepare something about the minister's life and problems, to be delivered as lectures at the Pastors' School of the California-Nevada Conference of the Methodist Church. The material was expanded for lectures at the Pastors' School of Methodism's Southern California-Arizona Conference. Invitations to do something of the same thing for the National Conference of Christian Work Among the Chinese in America and the Sacramento District Ministers' Retreat kept me at work on the ideas that are found here. A small amount of the material was first used in sermons in the First Methodist Church of Oakland, and a few paragraphs in Chapter VI were published in the *Pulpit Digest*, February, 1959, in an article entitled "The Revolt Against Togetherness."

Probably I am not unlike most people in writing a first book in that I required a good deal of encouragement. Without it, this work, modest as it is, would never have been completed or submitted to a publisher. For that reason I have an especially warm feeling of gratitude to Bishop Gerald Kennedy, Dr. Theodore A. Gill, Dr. John B. Magee, my brother ministers who heard the lectures and asked to see them in print, and the good laymen of the churches I have served who, for years, have been urging me to write a book.

In this connection, too, I must say a word of appreciation to my publisher, Harper & Brothers, whose relations with me were not at all what I had been led to expect—and fear—from a publisher. The kindness and encouragement I received have made me want to do my best.

Dr. Evelyn Miller Berger, Director of the East Bay Psychological Center; Dr. Herbert Otwell, Professor of Old Testament at the Pacific School of Religion; Dr. Colin Williams, until recently Professor of Historical Theology at Garrett Biblical Institute, and now teaching at Queen's College in Melbourne in his native Australia; and Dr. Robert W. Moon of the First Methodist Church of San Leandro, California, have all read the manuscript and made many helpful suggestions. They must not be held responsible for anything that I have said, but for the help they have given me I am grateful. Other friends, including my own Bishop, Donald H. Tippett, and Mrs. Tippett, have heard or read portions of the material, making suggestions that have improved it.

Not the least of the requirements of a writer is a quiet place in which to work. My thanks go to Gertrude and Harland Plummer for making their summer home in the mountains available to me while I was on vacation, and to Mr. Bruce R. Gates and the Y.M.C.A. of Oakland for a secluded room in the heart of a busy city.

Sharing the real burden of preparing the manuscript for publication have been my wife and my secretary. Mrs. Emily C. Willey disregarded working hours and personal weariness as she devoted herself to the task of producing a neat and accurate manuscript. In this endeavor she was assisted by my wife, Virginia, who has contributed far more to the book than the proofreading she did with such care. Most of the ideas expressed between these pages we have arrived at jointly during our years together in the ministry. And while I have been working on the book she has cheerfully carried much more than her share of family and even church responsibility, to give me time for writing. In this she had the full co-operation of the four younger Walkers, Jerry, Doug, Lois Ann, and Tommy, who, while surrendering a great deal of time they could rightly have claimed from their father, nevertheless worked their way into the pages of this book.

My deepest gratitude is extended also to the officials and members of the First Methodist Church of Oakland, California, who believe that if a minister is to do creative work he must be allowed the time to do it, and to the members of the church staff, who, during the time of preparation of this book, have carried more than their share of responsibility.

The Foreword was written by Bishop Gerald Kennedy. I am grateful to him for his friendship through the years, and for his willingness to have his name appear with mine on the jacket of a book about the ministry.

Biblical quotations are from the Revised Standard Version of the Bible, copyrighted 1946 and 1952 by the Division of Christian Education of the National Council of Churches of Christ in the U.S.A., and from J. B. Phillips' *The Gospels* (1957), *Letters to Young Churches* (1952), and *The Young Church in Action* (1955), published by The Macmillan Company. Unless otherwise indicated, it is to be understood that the quotation is from the Revised Standard Version. All Biblical quotations are used by permission of the publishers.

THE HUMAN PROBLEMS
OF THE MINISTER

I

CONDEMNED TO SIN PIOUSLY

❖ ❖ ❖

Recently a group of us attended a Convocation on Urban Life in America and considered "What the city does to people." Some of the effects of city living, we concluded, are loneliness, secularism, anonymity, materialism, and low moral standards. These are the problems our laymen encounter, and they deserve our sympathetic understanding.

But throughout our discussions, one thought kept pressing against my mind: ministers are not immune from their environment. What the city does to people it does to us. We are as involved in this caldron of modern evil as anyone.

The minister, like everyone else, is a sinner. Paul's letter to the Romans might well have been written to us: "What makes you think that you, who so readily judge the sins of others, can consider yourself beyond the judgment of God?" (Phillips) he asked. And again, "Prepared as you are to instruct others, do you ever teach yourself anything? You preach against stealing, for example, but are you sure of your own honesty? You denounce the practice of adultery, but are you sure of your own purity?" (Phillips). Ministers are as subject to temptation as anyone, and as likely to yield. As John Knox put it, "Demas is not the last minister who forsook his calling 'having loved this present world.'" Some men fall with a thud and surrender their parchments, but the rest of us, possibly more guilty because of our duplicity, continue both our preaching and our sinning.

Now to speak of ministers' sins in general terms seems less than forthright. Yet who could presume to enumerate all the evils of which one or more of us are guilty? Only God's mercy is wider than our guilt. Think of the fears we are ashamed to admit, our failure to come to terms with sex, our personal animosities, our careless handling of finances, our lack of faith, our thin devotional life, our strained family relations, our weaknesses as pastors, our impatience and our selfish ambition, to name only a few of our shortcomings. John Baillie has a more penetrating list:

My failure to be true even to my own accepted standards:
My self-deception in face of temptation:
My choosing of the worse when I know the better . . . :
My failure to apply to myself the standards of conduct I demand of others:
My blindness to the suffering of others and my slowness to be taught by my own:
My complacence towards wrongs that do not touch my own case and my over-sensitiveness to those that do:
My slowness to see the good in my fellows and to see the evil in myself:
My hardness of heart towards my neighbors' faults and my readiness to make allowance for my own:
My unwillingness to believe that [God] has called me to a small work and my brother to a great one.[1]

Sin is our common heritage. All of us have done things we had no business doing, and we have left undone those things we ought to have done. Bishop Ensley says, "There isn't any human being who could stand if God judged him by his deeds. If there is a hell, as our fathers believed, and the only way to escape it is by perfect conduct, we are all going to hell. There isn't any of us whose deeds are so pure that he can demand the right to go to heaven." We who lead our people in the prayer of communion, "We acknowledge and bewail our manifold sins and wickedness, which we from time to time most grievously have committed, by thought, word, and deed, against Thy Divine Majesty," are not speaking academically, nor are we putting words into the mouths of our people. We are speaking for ourselves, and inviting the congregation to join us.

Alan Walker tells of a woman who was struggling with alcoholism. Admitting that it took a good deal of courage to enter a church after being away from it for twenty years, she braced herself with a stiff brandy and entered the sanctuary. Explaining how she felt about the experience, she commented on how respectable the choir looked, and how she wondered if the usher who sat next to her would sit there if he knew how often she was drunk. Then she added, "I'm afraid I felt an intruder." No man's sin should make him an intruder among the rest of us, "since all have sinned and fall short of the glory of God." The minister, like everyone else, is a sinner.

But he isn't expected to be. And that's the rub! Because he preaches righteousness, it is anticipated that he lives it; what worse can be said about him than that he fails to practice what he preaches? Yet if our preaching never exceeds our practice, our people hear little to challenge them. There is small inspiration in hearing a man say, "This is what I do; be like me."

Nevertheless, most ministers feel a compulsion to exemplify the life they preach. In so far as this means an earnest striving to be better, it is good. But when it involves assuming righteousness that is not there, or hiding sins that are, it is evil. Pretense is one of our vocational hazards and suppressed guilt is our occupational disease. The layman can sin, and admit it, since no one expects him to be perfect anyway. If his mistakes pile up and become a heavy load of guilt, he can head for the minister's study, unburden the whole sorry mess, have a good cry, and go out with a spring and a whistle. But we preachers aren't supposed to be sinful, so how can we confess?

We are expected to have inner resources that keep life from getting us down, so no one would expect to find us in tears. The public builds up certain ideas about what a good minister should be, and we knock ourselves out to be what they think we are. When Sunday after Sunday a parade of people pass by us and say: "You spoke to my heart today," "It seemed you were speaking just to me," "I wish I understood life as you understand it," "You are the most Christlike person I have ever met," we are tempted to suspect we are as good as they say we are. Or, at least, we aren't about to reveal we are not— except for a suitably humble denial of their flattery, skillfully spoken so as to affirm it.

Because of the unique position the minister holds in the public eye, he finds it especially hard to handle his guilt. He runs a greater risk than the average person when he admits a sin, since his job seems to depend on people believing he is "going on to perfection." If he is overtaken in a trespass, he has little assurance that his brothers will "restore him in a spirit of gentleness," as Paul advised. If given a chance, they will make an attempt to, to be sure, but they may also get a good deal of satisfaction out of passing the tale of his shortcomings along to one another with whispered warnings not to tell. His ecclesiastical superiors are almost sure to find it out and keep it in mind when he comes up for a promotion. In addition, he runs the risk of his church people letting him down and rejecting him as their leader because of his "feet of clay." Neither his ecclesiastical superiors, his brother ministers, nor his parishioners are prepared to handle the "guilty" preacher.

So, being driven underground with our evil, we develop the art of sinning piously. We pass off our sins as virtues, and, because of the residue of "respect for the cloth" that still exists in our society, few people are brazen enough to call us on it. So we go merrily on our way, scrambling for the top of the greased pole of ambition by "accepting God's call to a larger field of service," enjoying more of the company of attractive widows than would be discreet if we were not there to "comfort them in their sorrow," and flaring out shamelessly at our opposition who are inhibiting "the progress of the Kingdom." Our failure to discipline ourselves we blame on "the heavy demands of the ministry"; our restless, purposeless leadership we excuse because our laymen "have no vision"; and our inadequacy as fathers and husbands we attribute to "the pressures of parsonage life." If the minister can't permit himself the luxury of a robust sin, no one can prevent him from spawning a mess of evil virtues.

A modern writer says of Gladstone that "his tendency was to believe that his desires were those of the Almighty. He was reproached, not so much for always having the ace of trumps up his sleeve as for claiming that God had put it there." The minister, too, is in danger of claiming divine sanction for behavior more congenial to the devil.

The Greek word for sin means, literally, "to miss the mark," and as Harold Walker points out, "Anybody can be forgiven for missing the mark, but to miss the mark and then to insist you hit it until you make yourself believe you did is unforgivable." He goes on to say:

The only sin you cannot conquer is the sin you will not admit, and the only sin God cannot forgive is the sin you dress up in the white robes of righteousness. Excuses and self-defense leave you with your sins compounded. Even an unintentional mistake becomes a sin when you try to defend it. But a mistake can turn into a source of strength when you face it fairly. Anybody will forgive an honest mistake honestly confessed, but nobody will forgive an honest mistake when you excuse it or deny it was a mistake.[2]

All of this is to say that we ministers do not handle our guilt satisfactorily by camouflaging it. This pious approach doesn't wash away our sins; it multiplies them by adding deception to the original offense. In his State of the Union Message to Congress in January, 1958, President Eisenhower said, "The world thinks of us as a country which is strong, but which will never start a war. The world also thinks of us as a land which has never enslaved anyone and which is animated by humane ideals." The first part of the statement is undoubtedly true. Most people in the world think of us as a strong country. But in connection with the rest of the statement one is tempted to ask. "Who is kidding whom?" There may be some who think of the United States as a country that will never start a war, but others are frightened to death that we will. Even some of our friends have expressed themselves as being more afraid that we would start a major war than that Russia would. And as for our being "a land which has never enslaved anyone," we'll leave it to the history books to clarify that. Certainly the rest of the world doesn't think of us as free from guilt. How much better it would have been if the President had said, "We are a country which is strong, but this increases the risk of our igniting a war. We acknowledge that slavery is a part of our history, and segregation is still a problem among us, but we want now to be animated by humane ideals." But the President is the President, and, rightly or wrongly, he undoubtedly feels that in his position he must admit nothing but righteousness. Actually, however, to say we have never enslaved anyone doesn't absolve us of our guilt; it merely adds to our offenses.

Now I have pointed out how this works in another area from our own so that we may see it more clearly as it applies to ourselves. Because of the position we hold, it is difficult for us to admit our own and our church's shortcomings; so we hide our sins, or close our eyes to them, or dress them in the garments of righteousness and thus multiply them, for guilt expands in the darkness.

It is for this very reason that we ministers, more than other people, need to unburden ourselves. Like a heavy trailer, too big for the car that pulls it, our past mistakes cling to our lives, slowing us down, decreasing our ability to move in traffic, burning up our energy. If only we could unhitch the trailer and free ourselves to do what we have always known we were capable of doing! But we cannot dismiss the load lightly. Our trailer is filled with the accumulations of a lifetime and it is always difficult to part with them, even when they are ugly; so, like the few personal items of furniture we carry from parsonage to parsonage just because they are ours, we take our past blunders with us to each new church we go to serve. Our compromises with conscience, our blunders in dealing with personnel, our cowardly failure to speak up, our desperate forcing of an advantage, our neglect of people who needed us, our skimping on our study, our substitution of intense activity for profound leadership, our jealousies and hatreds—these are the things that we would destroy if we could. But how can we?

We can do it the same way our laymen do—there is no other way—through the humble, even humiliating doorway of confession. There isn't a one of us who does not need to confess his sins. But to whom shall we go? To our wives or friends? (How objective can they be?) To another minister? (Do we dare?) To a psychiatrist or psychologist? (And admit the failure of "religion" to meet our needs?) To the Bishop? (When he, needing confession as badly as we, is no more likely to resort to it?)

Our dilemma is somewhat like that of one woman who put her feelings in verse:

I wish there were some one
Who would hear confession.
Not a priest—I do not want to be told of my sins;
Not a mother—I do not want to give sorrow;
Not a friend—she would not know enough;
Not a lover—he would be too partial;
Not a God—He is far away;
But some one who would be friend, lover, mother, priest, God,
    all in one,
And a stranger besides—who would not condemn or interfere;

Who, when everything is said from beginning to end,
Would show the reason of it all
And tell you to go ahead
And work it out your own way.[3]

The church ought to give that woman the opportunity for confession that she needs, but I am not sure it does. Neither is Jerome Ellison. He says, "Today the last place where one can be candid about one's faults is in church. In a bar, yes, in a church, no. I know; I've tried both places."

He does not, however, reject the church as the proper home of the confessing spirit. He says of the church, "I'll stick, and I'll keep saying, 'These are my faults, what are yours?' and at last there'll be three or four to respond and say, 'Why, these are mine, what shall we do about them?' and at once we few will be free from the awful effort of pretending to be worthy when we know we're not."

This is exactly the role we ministers must come to play in relation to each other. We must take seriously the counsel given by James: "You should get into the habit of admitting your sins to each other" (Phillips). The minister needs a minister just as a doctor needs a doctor. A physician once told me that it is a saying among medical men that the physician who prescribes for himself has a fool for a doctor and a fool for a patient. I have heard good physicians refer to "my doctor" and quote his instructions as freely as those of us who are not medically trained. This shows they believe in their profession. They have the confidence to put themselves in the hands of a brother physician when they need what only a doctor is trained to give. One staff of psychiatrists I know about turn to one another for professional help when they need to get themselves straightened out.

But what happens when a minister needs a minister? Does he have enough confidence in the training, the integrity, and the ability of his fellow clergy to put himself in their hands?

Usually not. Most of us spend a good deal of time talking about how important a minister is in the life of his people. We prepare and distribute brochures on when to call your minister, and what problems the minister is prepared to help solve. The pastor's column in a parish paper I read recently was devoted entirely to informing the laity that their minister was a professional counselor and fully qualified to help them with a variety of personal problems, a number of which were listed. Yet if that minister is typical of some I know, he would not admit he had problems of his own, nor, admitting them, would he be likely to appear at another minister's study with the expectation of finding help.

I know, of course, that there are exceptions to this. There are ministers who are not too proud to expose their shortcomings, and who have sufficient faith in their own profession to choose a fellow minister as their "father confessor." But such people are the exception and not the rule. The rest of us are too much identified with the vested interests of the ministry to risk the consequences.

If one is inclined to doubt this, let him ask himself a few pointed questions: To what brother minister would I feel free to go with a real problem? To which one would I confess the worst I know about myself? Have I in actuality gone to a minister as I like to think laymen come to me? If not, why not? Is it because I am beyond the need for this and have nothing to confess? Am I better than St. Francis, who always had something to confess to his brother monks? Why am I more proud of having people come to me to bare their souls than of having gone to someone else to do so myself? Which takes the greater courage, to hear a confession or to make one? Which does the most for one's growth? Is the felt need for confession a sign of weakness, or is it, perchance, an indication of strength? Is there a danger in hearing the stories of the lives of others while never quite releasing one's own?

Alcoholics Anonymous would not think of letting a man

counsel with another alcoholic unless he had first confessed his own inability to handle the problem alone. A qualified psychoanalyst has himself submitted to psychoanalysis; and if he is good at his job, he knows when it is time for him to sit in the counselee's chair again. The same thing applies to ministers. They must be confessers before they can be confessors.

Here is the principal reason ministers have not made a practice of going to one another with their burden of guilt. Who wants to be led through a dark and frightening tunnel by the hand of one who hasn't been through it himself? Ministers as a group have a compulsion to boast. This destroys their effectiveness as counselors to their brothers. Who wants to expose his failures and inadequacies, his mistakes and disappointments, to a man who has just told him his church is the fastest growing one in the conference and his Easter congregation was the biggest in years?

When I am failing in my ministry, I'm not buoyed up much by being shown a man who is a success; and when I am conscious of my sins, I get little help from the person who points out his own righteousness. In facing failure, I need the counsel of one who also has tried hard, and failed, but who knows there is victory even in a cross. In confronting my guilt, only harm can come to me from one who is "innocent." I need the help of one who is as guilty as I, but has experienced the glorious release of forgiveness that can come only to those who have experienced sin at first hand.

Now let's pause for a moment to pick up the thread we have been following. Everybody is sinful, and we ministers are no exception. We are in a unique position, however, in that we are expected to be righteous. This places us under particular strain which forces us to sin piously, to put a righteous cover on our shortcomings the way a clean tablecloth is put on top of a dirty one in the dining cars of trains. But this is no solution; it merely compounds our guilt, leaving us more than ever in need of release. The logical place to turn is to our brother ministers, but few of them show the kind of spirit that inspires our confidence; they give little evidence that they know much about confession.

What is the answer? It is to go at this thing together, to declare a moratorium on success stories, and begin to build our fellowship on the only firm foundation there is for any human fellowship: acknowledgment of our sins—not in the beautiful language of formal prayers only, but in the halting, stumbling, awkward words of those who, weary from the watch they've kept, unlock the gate behind which they have protected, defended, and tended their mistakes and blunders, and turn them loose to stand or fall in their own right. Only then can we gain the spiritual power this generation needs in its ministers. It is a mistake to suppose that confession is a sign of weakness. It is really an indication of strength. All men are weak, but the stronger ones know it and can bear to have it exposed while the weaker ones cover it up. It is the very willingness to admit the magnitude of one's error and one's helplessness to save himself that is the necessary prerequisite to effective living. Confession is not the last refuge of weaklings. It is not just an act of religious piety. It is an act of practical necessity for the one who would live a happy and useful life. The religious practice of confession was not set up arbitrarily by someone who happened to have a fancy to it. It was born out of experience; it was resorted to because generations of spiritual pilgrims have found out that it works. We are not told to confess our sins just to confess them, but because confession does something to us that we want done. "Only acknowledge your guilt," counsels the prophet Jeremiah. That's good counsel for ministers.

Other people admit their mistakes; why shouldn't we? When Mayor La Guardia of New York was confronted with the fact that the man he had appointed a judge on the municipal bench was a dishonest scoundrel, he did not try to justify his action. He merely said, "Boys, all I've got to say is this:

When I make a mistake it's a beaut." When Leroy Gore, a newspaper editor in Wisconsin, was challenged by a little girl to face up to the fact that in supporting Senator McCarthy he was supporting "government with lies," he admitted, "I was in a corner and I knew it," and added, "O.K., Jackie, you win. Hereafter we won't defend our democracy with lies if I have anything to say about it." And his newspaper courageously made an about-face. And an alcoholic testifies that he conquered his alcoholism only when "The kindness of God and man made it possible for me to admit wrong." And adds, "When I could admit it, I was spared the exhausting effort of trying to maintain the façade of phony bluster and pretense intended to conceal wrong, I became less tense, more relaxed, less afraid of people, more willing to help them."

We ministers need confession as badly as anyone, because it does something for us that nothing else can do. It completes the old business so that we can go on to the new. Did you ever attend a meeting where the time was used up with old business, rehashing things you had gone over before, and never getting around to the things still waiting to be done?

A sense of guilt is old business. It is made up of items that have not yet been disposed of. Every time one buckles down to being the kind of preacher and pastor he wants to be, and feels he ought to be, these items of unfinished business crowd in on the agenda to consume his energy and waste his time. Confession is the way to dispose of them and get them off the books.

This truth became dramatic in the story of the Prodigal Son and his brother. The Prodigal, clearly conscious of his errors, decided to confess to his father. He planned his speech in advance. "Father," he would say, "I have done wrong in the sight of Heaven and in your eyes. I don't deserve to be called your son any more. Please take me on as one of your hired men" (Phillips). With his approach carefully planned, he started home. But as he drew near, his father saw him coming and ran to meet him. As the two met, the boy began his speech, "Father, I have done wrong in the sight of Heaven and in your eyes. I don't deserve to be called your son anymore" (Phillips). But he never finished his speech! With a suddenness he could never in his remose have anticipated, the old business was done. The book was closed and new life opened to him. As the record says, "they began to make merry."

But his brother—whose sins, less blatant, remained without confession—stayed outside and sulked. New doors of adventure and joy did not open to him, because his pride and resentment were still first on the agenda. He had not completed his old business.

When a group of us were in Paris a guide took us to Notre-Dame Cathedral and told us by whose labor that great church was built. "As you know," he said, "Paris is a city of sinners. This church was built by them. They would come to confession and the priest would tell them that for this sin they would have to work three days on the Cathedral, and for that other sin they would be responsible for four days labor. And thus, confession by confession, the great Cathedral was built."

I do not know how many churches have been built that way. But I do know that ministers of good character are built, step by step, by the honest confessions of sinful men.

II

THE STRUGGLE TO LOVE OUR ENEMIES

❖ ❖ ❖

Everybody who is anybody has his enemies. There are people who irritate him, in whose presence he feels uncomfortable, whom he has a compelling urge to tell off.

A large portion of the population is free to express the urge. Politicians don't hide their animosity for one another. Businessmen know who their competitors are, and labor leaders know whom they are fighting.

But the Christian minister is in a different category. He is supposed to be nice. According to the popular superstition, he loves everybody, and goes about spreading sunshine and good will. He is not supposed to have any enemies, except, of course, the devil himself. It is not considered appropriate to his profession for him to show anger toward anyone, although, if he is generally well liked, he may be permitted a few expressions of "righteous indignation." It must be carefully explained, however, that he really loves the sinner; he is outraged only at the sin.

Now anyone with an ounce of experience in human relations knows that the offense cannot be so neatly severed from the offender. For all practical purposes a human being who does an obnoxious thing is an obnoxious human. And so long as he persists in doing it he is an enemy to be dealt with and not just "a nice person whom we need to understand." In his *Days of Our Years*, Pierre van Paassen tells of a parish priest who was outraged at the behavior of members of

14

his congregation. Stepping into the pulpit on one occasion, he addressed them as follows: "Christians!" And van Paassen says the word had the effect of a whiplash. He said it again: "Christians! When the Lord of life and death shall ask me on the Day of Judgment, 'Pasteur de la Roudaire, where are thy sheep?' I will not answer Him. And when the Lord shall ask me for the second time: 'Pasteur de la Roudaire, where are thy sheep?' I will yet not answer Him. But when the Lord shall ask me the third time: 'Pasteur . . . de . . . la . . . Rou . . . daire, where . . . are . . . thy . . . sheep?' I shall hang my head in shame and I will answer: They were not sheep, Lord—they were a pack of wolves!'"[1]

Not many ministers are called to shepherd an entire pack of wolves, but rare indeed is the man who does not have at least a few members whose behavior is bestial. Often they find their way into key positions and exercise a sinister control over church policy and procedure. They like to get on finance committees where they can control the purse strings, or on nominating committees where they can determine personnel, or on the pastoral relations committee where they can dominate the preacher himself. You may call them anything you like—characters, obstructionists, or tireless workers and devoted churchmen—but any minister who has tried to work with them knows they are his enemies, the people with whom, in meeting after meeting, telephone conversation after telephone conversation, and nightmare after nightmare, he is compelled to do battle.

One can never predict in advance where the enemy will show himself. We have already mentioned certain areas of church responsibility that commonly draw troublemakers. But they show up in other places. Sometimes a minister's worst enemies are on his staff. Taking advantage of his compulsion to be "nice" to everyone and his reluctance to do anything to hurt anybody, some of them are capable of imposing on him unmercifully. Because he does not want to precipitate an unpleasant incident, many a minister has limped along with incompetent and even disloyal staff members. Outwardly he accepts them, but there is an inner rejection which reduces his own efficiency and cripples the effectiveness of staff teamwork.

A minister may also find enemies among his ecclesiastical superiors. Often a man rebels against the high-handed methods used by some offensive denominational leaders, but in the interest of Christian harmony—and his own ministerial security—he sits on his boiling resentments and quietly fumes.

Some enemies of the minister are outside the church itself and in the community at large. A newspaper editor may give him a bad time, or a politician may challenge him.

These enmities take different forms. Some of them break out in open opposition. Occasionally one encounters a layman who is opposed to his minister and doesn't care who knows it. A church-school teacher may flatly refuse to use the material in the new curriculum which the minister has been promoting or an irate member may choose an important board meeting as the proper setting for condemning the preacher's sermons or his methods of pastoral work. Sometimes this open opposition can split a church, but usually it is not too damaging. When a hothead breaks into the open, he reveals his hand and the people see him for the unstable person he is. If the minister maintains his composure, sympathy is likely to find its way to his side of the controversy.

The minister's more serious enemies, however, are those who do their work subtly. They have several characteristic ways of operating. One is to sit through an important meeting without a word of opposition to the program that is being projected, and then in the succeeding days to plant doubts and raise objections in the minds of everyone with whom they carry on a conversation. Another subtle form of opposition is to compliment the minister highly, praise him for his ideas, and conclude by saying with a father-knows-best air, "but we are not in a position to do it now." Still other enemies of the minister pose as his friends and talk endlessly about supporting and helping him. Probably they think that is exactly what they are doing, but in reality they are offending his personality by attempting to reshape him to fit the pattern of his predecessor or of some image of the ideal minister which they have in their own minds. They treat their preacher with the same loving care a wife extends to the husband she has married to reform.

Clearly the minister is in a different position. Like anyone else, he has his enemies; but unlike most, he feels compelled to pretend they are his friends. In part this is due to popular opinion that shapes his profession into a stereotype. In part it is due to his own sincere desire to be a true follower of the One who counseled men to love their enemies. Our question now is how a minister can handle his enmities constructively. We'll look first at some inadequate solutions to the problem.

One is suppression. This leads to bottled rage with its conglomerate litter of offspring. Psychologists agree that suppressed hatred is unhealthy. If it does not lead directly to some organic ailment, at least it upsets emotional stability and points toward neurotic behavior. It causes nervousness, insecurity, biased judgment, and an inefficient use of energy. It may even lead to dishonesty.

Under pressure, ministers are likely to become crafty. Shrewdly they lay their plans to short-circuit the work of a committee, cover up a blunder, or give an impression that is contradictory to the facts. It isn't that they are fundamentally dishonest. It is just that their anger has reached a higher voltage than they are equipped to carry. They don't feel free to express it directly, so they siphon it off in other ways.

Some years ago the nation was shocked by news of the brutal murder of a girl named Marian Baker. Richard Gehman, who sought to understand what motivated the youth who committed this crime, comments,

He was not merely killing her. All his life, women had loomed over him as vicious symbols of authority, tantalizing, shadowy mistresses who controlled him and yet who taunted him by remaining ever out of grasp. While they used him as they wished, they whispered that he could dominate them—but he could not. They were too tricky, too elusive, too ultimately unattainable. Every mundane problem confronting him on the afternoon of January tenth was in some way connected with a woman. He could not bear it. The hostility, festering perhaps from the time he had been trained to the toilet, screamed for release. He did not simply kill Marian Baker. He killed his mother, teachers in school who had twisted him into learning, nurses in the Army hospital, whores in Italy, laughing and witless Pitman girls, his wife, his wife's friends, his friends' wives and girls, girls he saw on Lancaster and Pitman streets, girls he observed while at work in his various part-time jobs, every girl and every woman he had hated and simultaneously wanted. He murdered them all.[2]

This is an extreme expression of suppressed rage. I don't know of any minister who has indulged in such an impulse slaying, although a search of the records might disclose one. But I do know men who have blown up on the job and asked for a transfer, or have suddenly left the ministry without being sure why. I wonder if in rejecting the ministry as a vocation they are rejecting the man who stood in the way of granting a much-deserved raise, the woman who forced the committee to settle for a used davenport for the parsonage living room, the superintendent who recommended them for the smaller church instead of the big one, and all the rest of the difficult people they had the urge to oppose, but never quite did.

A second inadequate solution to ministerial enmity is submission. I once knew a woman who claimed that she and her husband had never quarreled. I thought this was something of an achievement until I visited in their home. There I observed that the only thing that had been achieved was the submission of a husband to his wife. Similarly, travelers returning from Russia often report that while the satellites are populated with embittered people who resent the oppression under which they live, the people of Russia itself seem relaxed and happy. This is because most of them have adjusted to their Communist dictatorship by submitting to it.

Some ministers face opposition in their churches in this same manner. They just buckle under. Refusing to engage in a quarrel with any of their people, they adjust as best they can to the dominant person. In doing this they abdicate their position as chief administrative officer of their church, and become the tool of a stronger personality. They may save themselves the rigor of controversy, but they sacrifice their souls. No man called to the ministry of One who accepted a cross has any business rejecting his own hour of conflict for the precarious harmony of submission.

Another inadequate way of dealing with one's enemies is avoidance. Often when a small child becomes angry with his playmate, he just goes home. His "I won't play with you any more" is a natural enough way for a child to meet the frustration of clashing wills. But some adults use the same method. Taking seriously the advice that the only way to get along with some people is to get along without them, they stay away from gatherings where they will be thrown into association with those they don't like. They solve their interpersonal relations by walking on the other side of the street, resigning from the committee, or transferring to another church. Or they may continue to see the person but avoid the subject which involves tension.

This latter method enables them to continue in the company of people who seem objectionable to them, but it doesn't represent much of an accomplishment. Some people take it as a matter of course that if they want to keep their friends they must stay away from certain subjects involving controversial issues. This has always seemed to me to reveal a superficial concept of friendship. In my judgment friendship is synonymous with the freedom to talk about anything you like. If a man wants to bridle my tongue, he isn't my friend.

Unfortunately many ministers almost never feel free to say what they really think when they are with the members of their own church. They choose their words with care, always taking into account the potential reactions of the particular persons present. But this is no way to live; it is the way people exist in an enemy camp. A friend of mine spent several months in a subterranean prison in East Germany. He said that he would be interrogated all night long, and when he failed to give the desired answers, he was kicked and beaten. "What did you do during the day?" I asked. He said he slept a little but most of the time he tried to anticipate what questions would be asked him the next night to be sure that in his weakness he would not be caught off guard and say the wrong thing.

That is normal enough behavior for a prisoner. But it is neither natural nor right for a minister of the gospel to guard what he says to his own people for fear of bringing on some kind of persecution.

A fourth inadequate method of dealing with enemies is rudeness. There are times when one is called on to confront his opponents directly, or even bluntly, but there is never an excuse for being rude.

In July, 1958, a western newspaper carried an article with a New York dateline, entitled "Wagner to Give Khrushchev the Saud Snub." The article said in part, "Mayor Robert F. Wagner, who snubbed Saudi Arabia's King Saud when the latter visited New York early last year, also will omit welcome to Nikita Khrushchev if the Soviet Premier comes here for a summit conference, he said today."

It is an immature person who can think of no better way to win his enemies to his point of view than to snub them. Rudeness convinces few people of the superiority of one's way of life.

Yet, regrettably, there are ministers who are inexcusably rude to people who seem to be causing them trouble. They force them out of key positions without so much as the courtesy of an explanation; they violate the sanctity of the pulpit by making veiled remarks that are aimed to wound their adversary; and, like the Mayor, they extend the cordiality of their office with a snub.

Probably they think this is all for the good of the Kingdom. But it is worth noting that one of the keys to the success of the famed Montgomery bus strike was the Negroes' rejection of rudeness as an acceptable attitude toward one's enemies. The leaders of the strike insisted on a dignified approach, and in meeting after meeting indoctrinated their people on the importance of common courtesy. Sometimes at their meetings a speaker would become carried away with himself, and lash out with abusive language against the whites. One minister wound up a tirade by referring to certain whites as "dirty crackers." But Martin Luther King reports, "After the meeting he was politely but firmly informed that his insulting phrases were out of place."

Rudeness is always out of place in the Christian ministry.

Now, having commented on some inadequate methods of dealing with one's enemies, I want to describe what may constitute a sane approach for the Christian minister who is forced to deal with a variety of people who seem, either by deliberate intent or awkwardness and blundering, to make his life a misery.

His first responsibility is to face the situation honestly. A minimum of personal integrity requires him to admit the existence and the extent of his enmity. He will never learn to love his enemies by pretending they don't exist or that they don't irritate him. The only way to develop a healthy love for your enemy is to find a robust enemy who makes loving a real challenge. Jesus never said, "Don't have any enemies." He said, "Love your enemies." Obviously you can't love somebody who doesn't exist, or who you pretend doesn't exist. To assume one has no enemies may be only an escape mechanism to avoid the painful discipline of loving them.

It is likely that any effective minister will be popular with some, but there will be others whom he will upset. It often comes as a shock to people when they learn there are those who do not like them. It may be nothing more than a clash of personalities, or it may be they are disliked for a stand they have taken, or convictions they hold. But whatever the cause, anyone who amounts to anything has his enemies. It is no compliment to say that everybody loves him. Jesus said, "Woe unto you when all men speak well of you." If a man stands for anything he is bound to have his opponents.

As Bishop Kennedy puts it, "The important thing is to have the right enemies." And he adds, "It has always been a source of profound satisfaction for me to know that when I was transferred to another city, some people were greatly relieved."

After facing up to the fact that even he can have enemies, the minister should take a square look at the offender to see if he is really what he appears to be. Most people put on one kind of front or another, and a good many of their actions are compensatory. If one can get behind the mask, he may find the real person to be quite delightful. Initial feelings of repulsion may change to sympathy when the facts emerge; all of us have had the experience of growing unusually fond of a person whom, at the outset, we thoroughly disliked. The minister should make every effort to distinguish a true enmity from a spurious one. Resenting a person who is really playing on his team is a regrettable misuse of emotion.

My initial reaction to one young woman who came to a church I was serving was that she was a negative personality and would have a depressing effect on any group she was associated with. I couldn't have been more mistaken. She wasn't negative, she was just frightened. Not the glad-hander who barges into a new group calling everyone by his first name after an hour's acquaintance, she had to feel sure of herself before her true personality traits were revealed. As it turned out, she was highly intelligent, had a keen wit, was an excellent piano player, and was one of the most capable people I have seen at leading group singing.

My first real encounter with a professor in one of my churches was when he told me what he thought of the ineffectiveness of the missionary committee on which he was serving. If we couldn't plan a more constructive program than he had seen evidenced so far, he wasn't interested in wasting his time with it. If I had just assumed he was a "knocker," and had argued the effectiveness of what really was a rather weak committee, I would have made one of the worst mistakes of my ministry. Instead, I asked him, as we began a new year, to assume chairmanship of the committee. I have never seen anyone do a better job. He wasn't a professional church complainer at all. He was a highly capable person who was impatient with inefficiency, and was not challenged by small ideas and weak programs. All he needed was a big job to challenge his own unusual ability. He had never done a job like this before, but later he said laughingly, "I figured if the minister was crazy enough to ask me to do it, I was crazy enough to try." Almost overnight he became one of the best church leaders I have ever had the privilege of working with.

But this is not to say that all people who seem objectionable are really swell fellows if you get to know them. Some of them are troublemakers from the beginning, and after the minister has satisfied himself that they are doing the church and its work more harm than good, he should proceed to deal with them by whatever method seems most appropriate. In the meantime, let him remember that the majority of his members are wonderful folks who wish him well. He should beware of the temptation to let a few difficult personalities color his attitude toward an entire church. It is so frighteningly easy to fall into the error of saying, "The laymen are critical of everything I do," or "The members of this church are really hard to work with," when what is really meant is, "There are two or three people in this church who inhibit progress and stir up opposition." It is far better to single out the offenders and discipline them than to damn an entire church membership because of the behavior of a few.

In the meantime, let the minister heed the advice of Paul to think of things that are lovely and of good report. The other day my wife was talking about a fine couple in our church, and suddenly she broke forth into spontaneous tribute. She said, "They are wonderful people. You automatically think good thoughts when you see them." The minister should remember he has members like that as well as the ones who stimulate a darker mental image.

Another thing that honest evaluation requires of the minister is that he take a square look at his own emotional equipment. It may be that he stimulates enmity. People who have worked harmoniously enough with other ministers may find him hard to get along with. He may have some irrational aversions which alienate him from certain types of people. He may compensate for his own feelings of insecurity by a tendency to dominate. When this arouses antagonism, he should recognize that *he* is the true aggressor, not the layman. If he secretly despises the people, they will sense this and be unfriendly to him. If he is afraid of them, and tries with excessive dedication to cater to their needs, they will come to despise him, and there will be trouble. Only a deep respect for persons, for what they are capable of becoming, and for the love that God has extended toward them is a proper basis for building a solid relationship with one's parishioners.

But something more than respect is necessary. It is something that probably falls under the heading of public relations. At any rate, if a minister is going to take an honest look at the situation, he should not fail to find out what his people think of him. What is the image they have of their minister? Just

as a minister can be mistaken in his judgment about laymen.
they can have a very wrong idea about him. Speaking of the
very "offensive portrait" of Disraeli which the people of England had of the young statesman, André Maurois writes, "The
young Disraeli would have been greatly surprised if he had met
himself as an Englishman in the City might have imagined
him at that time. He would have kept the creature at arm's
length, with horror and scorn; he would not have doubted that
he had just met the most redoubtable enemy he would hence-
forth have to fight."[3]

I suspect that many of us would be horrified if we could
catch a glimpse of ourselves as some of our laymen see us.
Probably we would agree with the laymen that what they are
looking at is really an objectionable creature. Our job then becomes the difficult one of persuading them that the image they
have is a false one. We really are not what they have come to
think we are. When they see us as we are, they will like us
better.

After he has made every effort to understand the problem—
his "enemy," himself, and the total situation—the minister
should determine his strategy for dealing with the enemy and
transforming the enmity. There are no methods that are 100
per cent effective, and a plan that would be useful in one
instance would be quite out of place in another. There is a
sense in which every minister is on his own when it comes to
meeting problems like these. He has to play it by ear. No script
is written that will meet the emergency, and even his original
speeches, composed in advance of an encounter with a real
troublemaker, will likely prove to be artificial and quite useless.
When on the battlefield he must make his own decisions; with
the scrip thrown away, he must ad-lib.

Nevertheless, there are certain basic strategies which are
useful in some instances, and everyone should familiarize
himself with them.

The first is to learn from your enemy by making him your

teacher. One way to win those who dislike us is to listen seriously to their criticism, and institute some personal reforms along the lines they suggest. A man's enemies have an uncanny ability to locate his weak spot. If their campaigns against him are effective, it is usually because their charges are based on a certain amount of truth. Recognizing this fact, E. Stanley Jones once said, "My critics are the unpaid watchmen of my soul." All of us want to be better ministers than we are, but we aren't always sure where to begin. There is no one who can tell us better than those who dislike us.

The difficulty is, however, that we don't want to take it from them. When they criticize us, we react, almost automatically, by denying the criticism and, perhaps, by directing some well-chosen and sharp words at their weak spots for good measure. Of course, that only increases the tension and exaggerates the problem. If we would seriously try to win our enemies, we should learn to accept their criticism more graciously.

The point is illustrated in the lives of politicians. One once said, "I never read the men who are against me." Others have made it almost a sacred ritual of the day to read the newspapers that are their bitterest critics. If they know what the opposition is saying against them, they know how to change their ways to win them. Similarly, many business concerns go to a great deal of trouble to get suggestions from those who are displeased with the services rendered. They ask for criticisms.

There is nothing, I take it, that will win the opposition faster than for them to see we are reforming ourselves at the very points where they have criticized us. It makes them feel we respect them enough to listen to what they have said; it makes them respect us to see us put our pride in our pockets, admit we have made some mistakes, and change our ways. There is a text in the Book of Acts that puts this truth better than I can. Peter and John had been boldly teaching their gospel among the people, although many condemned them and said they were false leaders. Then they proved their power by healing a man, and the record says of the people that, "seeing the man that had been healed standing beside them, they had nothing to say in opposition." One way to silence our enemies is to improve our preaching, enrich our calling, strengthen our administration. And when they see a man who has been healed standing before them, there will be little left to say in opposition.

A second possible approach is a direct attack. It would be unwise to use this method in many instances, but in some it is the best possible solution. There are some troublemakers who do not understand subtleties, and who are unresponsive to reason. It is a psychological problem with them. They get an idea in their heads and it won't come out except by a severe shaking. Some of them are bold and accusative; some are dull and persistent; and some are sweet with a "modesty" that covers a sharp sword. But as different as they are, they have one thing in common: they needle the minister, and they never give up until their unkindness is thrown in their face with a directness that would be rude if extended to anyone else.

It is not rude to deal firmly with these people, any more than it is rude for a parent to give a sound spanking to a misbehaving child. And just as a child in a loving household where no spankings are delivered except for good cause is observably happier after he has paid the full price for his errors, so these people normally become more relaxed and co-operative after they have been boldly told off.

There is good precedent for this approach. Jesus is reported to have accented his words with a whip when he told one group of men that the temple had put up with them long enough. They had worn out his patience. The time was past for reasoning or suggesting they might like to try a different job, or talking about co-operation. It was time to talk up to them and make it abundantly clear they were out of line. Jesus was indignant with the men in the temple, and he didn't hide his indignation from them.

We have a badly distorted view of Jesus if we do not see this side of him. There may have been times when he could fit the "Gentle Jesus, meek and mild" stereotype, but there is less evidence of this than that he was a bold man of God who could put up with stupidity and greed only so long before speaking up.

Review the record again, and see the indignation that more than once rose to the surface. "Get behind me, Satan," he said to one of his best friends one day, when the disciple had made a remark that was meant only in kindness. Mark refers to a time when "he looked around at them with anger," and Luke records a message he sent to Herod with instructions to tell it to "that fox." He called the scribes and pharisees "whitewashed tombs" and "serpents," and told the arrogant, self-righteous folk that the harlots would get into heaven before they would. So you see, it is quite in keeping with his spirit that he should step into the temple and begin to reform things. And it was no mild reformation. As Arthur John Gossip in *The Interpreter's Bible* puts it, "This was a wild scene, with cowering figures clutching desperately at their tables, as these were flung here and there; or running after their spilled coins, as these rolled hither and thither; or shrinking from the lash that had no mercy till the holy place was cleansed." It seems evident that when Jesus staged a reform, he went about it with a firm hand.

Of course no minister is called on to play God, or to carry a whip because Jesus used one. It seems evident from Jesus' actions, however, that there is nothing in the Christian faith to require one to buckle under to the difficult personalities who are sometimes to be found in churches. Rather, there is reason to believe that the time comes when they are to be handled with firmness. The woman who drives people away from the church with her constant complaining should be told *good* outright that she is hindering the work of the church and has got to stop. The man who threatens to cancel his pledge if a particular building plan is accepted should be encouraged to cancel it. And the person who holds onto a key position without doing what the job requires should be replaced even if his feelings are hurt. A part of his maturing is to learn that while the church is made up of people who are quite willing to accept him in spite of his weaknesses, they are not required to sacrifice their church's program to his procrastination and inefficiency.

To put it simply, coddling and nonresistance are not the methods to be used in dealing with the troublemakers that are to be found in every church. Such methods are hard on everybody, including the offender. This is something the lay people need to understand. Many of the finest have the mistaken notion that Christian practice requires them to pamper the temperamental and cater to the whims of the neurotic. They expect their minister to do the same. But this merely encourages these people in their immaturities. The best way to cure a child of whining, sulking, or temper tantrums (whether the child is four or forty-four) is to make it evident that this behavior doesn't get him what he wants.

A word of caution needs to be spoken here. A high measure of emotional stability and personal humility must be a part of the minister's own make-up if he is going to make this method work. Even firmness must be wrapped in love if it is to be redemptive. The direct approach loses its power when it is an expression of arrogance. And the resolution of an angry man to be firm with his opponent is suspect. There is always the possibility that the minister himself is the true enemy of what the church is trying to accomplish. When this is the case, it is the responsibility of some layman to apply the technique we have been describing to the man he calls his pastor. A minister has no more right than a layman to impose his eccentricities on a congregation, and no fancied respect for the cloth should prevent a mature layman from telling him so.

A third approach the Christian minister can make to his enemies is aggressive good will. While there are some people who seem to need a psychological spanking before they can get hold of themselves, what most people need is appreciation, affection, and praise. Love is not the only power that can work for good, but it is still the greatest, and it is an appropriate instrument in the hands of the minister.

This is too obvious to labor. Every minister knows it is important to love his enemies; he has been preaching sermons on this theme since the day he first stepped into the pulpit. To be sure, he has had his difficulties translating his words into works, but if he has any real doubt about the power of love he is in the wrong vocation and ought to make an adjustment without delay.

When a college girl from California visited an orphanage in Japan, one little boy approached her hopefully with the question, "Are you going to be my Mommy?" "No," she said. "I'm sorry." Then he asked, "Will you kiss me anyway?" Another child of an orphanage is reported to have slipped a note through the fence that surrounded the institution where he lived. The message read, "Whoever finds this, I love you."

I know nothing about the behavior pattern of these two children. About all I know is that they were human, and were giving an unsophisticated expression to their need to be loved. As people grow older their tongues tend to be tied. Inhibitions prevent them from speaking of their real needs as candidly as did the children. So they speak in a different language, much less winsome and more difficult to understand. They act out their story in little dramas, neatly staged to conceal the message they are trying to put over. When a man stands up in a board meeting to oppose vigorously what seems like a constructive program, he may not really be an obstructionist, but only an overlooked member making his bid for attention. When another visits the pastor's study to challenge the minister on something said in a sermon, he may not dislike the minister. It is possible he likes him very much and wishes for some sign that the feeling is mutual. These people need love more than they need reprimanding. They need to feel they count for something.

Most of us are not effective at meeting this need. As a matter of fact, the average minister thinks he is more loving than he is. A friendly smile and an air of good will toward all of God's children is an enviable trait in a minister, but it does not necessarily meet the deeper need of the human heart for real understanding and caring. As one member said of his pastor, "He gives the impression of being warmhearted and friendly, but he has never been really close to anyone." Love for an enemy is something more than the absence of overt conflict; it is more than a friendly greeting with its "and how is your sweet wife and those wonderful children?" It is know-ing the enemy; it is feeling what he feels; it is acceptance of him in spite of his actions or personality traits; it is the initiative to be with him conquering the impulse to avoid him; it is the acceptance of the hurt he inflicts; it is understanding of the forces that shape his personality; and it is faith that God's redeeming power can work through you and through him. To love your enemy is not to affirm an affection which doesn't exist. It is to act on the conviction that all of God's children are to be respected.

To put it differently, the minister should make sure that his enemy isn't treated as an enemy. Martin Niemoeller put it right when he said, "It took me a long time to learn that God is not the enemy of my enemies. He is not even the enemy of His enemies." The challenge is to be a friend to our enemies.

This is the attitude the minister should have toward the wolves that invade his flock. But it is a mistake to suppose he is the only one who should have it. There is no reason why he has to provide the full quota of human affection for each disturbed member. When the idea gets around that only the minister can meet the need of these people, something basic in Protestantism has been offended. The minister must set the example, but there are often laymen who are in a better position to do the job than the minister is. The goal should be the building of a church that is itself a loving, redemptive fellowship in whose warm embrace the "enemy" thaws out and becomes human. It is the climate of loving concern which the minister must be instrumental in developing.

Hanns Lilje worked on this even in the unpromising environment of a prison cell. He tells how he always said "Thank you" to the guards for their daily routine, such as putting a water jug outside his cell or giving him a clean towel. These words often opened the door to more serious conversation. On at least one occasion they all but upset the equilibrium of the guard to whom they were addressed. It was shortly after the practice of chaining men to their bunks at night was established. When an elderly guard came in and fastened his fetters, Lilje said politely, "Thank you very much." This is the way he describes what followed: "He stood still and stared at me; then he went out of the cell; and in a moment or two he came back again, and said in an awkward, rough voice: 'No need to thank me for a thing like that!' I replied: 'Well, you have only done your duty!'—an expression dear to the heart of any good German official! If he had not lost the power of expressing emotion and tenderness, he would have done so now, but this was beyond him, so shaking his head he strode out of the room, murmuring to himself."[4]

Kindness and respect extended toward one who neither deserves nor expects it is a powerful instrument for disposing of one's enemies. It can make them friends.

I want to mention one more method by which a minister can learn to love his enemies. This is the simple device of finding another, more potent enemy whom you can unite in opposing. During World War II, Communist Russia almost became our friend as we joined forces to combat a common enemy. And even now there are grounds for hoping that our joint endeavor to abolish war and conquer space may turn our angry eyes from one another to a foe that is really worth conquering. If a minister and his most irritating troublemakers can be yoked together in a common effort, points of enmity may become dulled, even if they do not completely disappear.

And of course this is precisely the function of the church—or at least a function of the church—to unite the forces of sincere Christians in the ever-raging battle with evil. We must never forget that, annoying as some of our church members or ecclesiastical superiors can be, they are never the real enemy; and when our minds are too much occupied by questions of how to handle them, we are taking leave of our primary function. Indeed, there is the strong possibility that such internal enmities arise because we have already taken leave of it. People without a purpose are more likely to aim their aggression at one another than are those who have an urgent job to do. The happiest and most peaceful church congregations are not those that have done the best job of settling scores between the members, but those that are on the warpath. No one with any spunk is happy unless he is fighting a battle. Maturity is found in the wisdom to choose which battle to fight.

It was in this spirit that Martin Luther King, Jr., distinguished the true enemy from the false one in the Montgomery bus strike. He said to his people, "The tension in this city is not between white people and Negro people. The tension is, at bottom, between justice and injustice, between the forces of light and the forces of darkness. And if there is a victory, it will be a victory not merely for fifty thousand Negroes, but a victory for justice and the forces of light. We are out to defeat injustice and not white persons who may be unjust."[5]

We Christians have a big job to do, and we must put all our strength into the effort. There is a war to be won against hunger, disease, oppression, ignorance, fear, hatred, and all else that is an offense to God and contrary to his will. Surely anyone who is willing to join us in this battle is our friend.

III

COMPETING WITH OUR BROTHERS

❖ ❖ ❖

After Carl Austin Hall had kidnapped Bobby Greenlease, murdered him, buried the body in a shallow grave, and collected the ransom, he began to feel important. He had always wanted wealth with the power it gives to the man who possesses it, and at last he had accomplished his purpose. Riding in a cab with his suitcase full of money, he confided to the driver that he hated little people. "I want to be big," he said.

The thing that he did was despicable. Few of us would be guilty of such brutality. Yet in his motivation we can catch a glimpse of ourselves. We, too, want to be big. To be sure, we may have no desire to be the President of the United States, or the richest man in the world, but we want to be more important than we are and we want to possess more money than we have. Once when the senior Rockefeller was asked how much wealth it takes to satisfy a man, he answered, "Just a little more."

The climb toward the top seems to be an accepted part of civilization. If one doesn't give evidence in his profession that he is advancing, something is considered to be wrong. This is as true in the ministry as in other vocations. Rare indeed is the man who, upon graduation from seminary, does not set his sights on a large and important parish. A little later he comes to terms with the fact that he may have to settle for a smaller church off the beaten track, but at any rate he's definitely on the way up, and if promotions do not come quickly he grows nervous.

Most of us have deplored the way in which young business-men, greedy to make another dollar or to gain an advance-ment, neglect their church, devoting even their Sundays to their work. We have preached sermons about it. But we needn't appear so self-righteous! We give seven days a week to our job too often for similar reasons. We are ambitious. Busy making a name for ourselves in the profession, we have little time for worship we are not conducting for someone else, and none at all for the traditional day of rest.

Ministers, like everyone else, are engaged in a scramble for the top. One sports writer put it bluntly: "The clergy is more concerned with going through the chairs of the hierarchy than with peace on earth, good will toward men." And John Knox, recognizing the dangers of pride in position, wrote, "It is as hard for the so-called big preacher to enter the kingdom of heaven as for any other successful man or woman—probably harder."

We spend a good deal of time selling ourselves. If we are to get to the top, our exceptional qualities will have to be known. Sometimes we pass the word along through subtle, humble-sounding, but well-timed comments about the work we are doing, and sometimes, especially when the situation is more desperate, we give way to unrestrained boasting. Our wives often help us in this. In order that the illusion of our modesty may be preserved, they are often kind enough to be our mouthpiece. "My husband is too modest to tell you this," they begin, absolving us of any taint of pride, and then they recite the impressive record of our most recent accomplish-ments.

On other occasions, we seek to raise our own stock by criticizing the work that someone else is doing, or allowing our praise of him to be too obviously restrained. The most reserved compliments on a man's preaching are likely to come from his brother ministers. We are all terribly afraid of overrating the other fellow or giving him the impression we think he is doing a better job than we.

This restrained enthusiasm for our brother's preaching is a mystery to our laymen, who, feeling no sense of competition, are free to "receive a blessing" from any reasonably effective sermon without feeling compelled to judge technique and pass on theological nuances. Thus a layman may say to me, after a sermon we have both heard, "Wasn't that a wonderful sermon? That man surely can preach!" And I am likely to answer with the air of a practiced connoisseur, "Oh, it was all right, I guess—better than some, but he didn't really lift my spirit." Of course he didn't. I wouldn't let him. If I should admit that he had the capacity to reach my spirit, I would be admitting he was a great preacher, and his being a great preacher would be a threat to my status.

Another way we have of gaining status for ourselves is by singling out our particular kind of ministry for special emphasis. For nine years I served a college church responsible for the work of the Wesley Foundation. During that time I attended many meetings of student workers. They were ordinary men and women, no more and no less capable than the general run of pastors in our churches. Some of them were outstanding, but others were definitely limited in their capabilities. I've gone through the application papers of several dozen applicants for the position of minister to students, and exceptional people are as rare here as in any other field. Nevertheless, some of them are intoxicated with a sense of their own superiority. With a sophomoric adulation of the college campus, they seek self-importance by identification with the institution in our society that is considered to be intellectual.

But there is a reason for this. Generally speaking, the student worker is forced to fight for his position in his denomination. He is often overlooked as other men from local churches are advanced beyond him. Frequently, his name is left off crucial mailing lists, and he finds himself uninformed about important matters that affect all the clergy. Working as he does with students, he is sometimes identified with the "kids" and thought of as only a youngster. It is not surprising, therefore, that when he gathers at meetings with others of his kind, he should be somewhat on the defensive, and welcome the chance to sing in chorus with his compatriots, "We think we are pretty fine."

Coming from a student church to a city church, I discovered another group that find it to their advantage to praise their particular brand of ministry. The "downtown ministers" tend to think of themselves as the top men. I meet regularly for lunch with the downtown ministers of my city. They are fine men, and I enjoy their company. But I think there is something significant about the fact that they make it a point to include the senior ministers only, and to confine the constituency to the large downtown churches. To be sure, we have certain things to talk about that would not be important to men in the outlying churches, and many of the things they would bring up for discussion would be quite irrelevant to our situations. But it is also true that we are the big boys, and we like to get together to tell one another that.

In this regard, we are not altogether unlike my four-year-old son. One day, when I had occasion to comment to him on how good his big brothers had been, he said, "They're not good. There are just three good people: Jesus, and God, and me."

The simple truth is that most ministers have a heavy quantity of ego in their personalities. Like Carl Austin Hall, they want to be big. Each man is out to get as close to the top as his abilities and a reasonable adherence to the principle of Christian humility will let him.

Yet the ministry is a brotherhood. It is as rich a fellowship as you can find anywhere on earth. When clergymen get together there will be fun. No tricks of group work are necessary to break down the reserve and get the men talking with one another; laughter is spontaneous and singing is hearty. It is a thrilling thing to be in a fellowship like this.

But this very fact is a part of our problem and contributes to the inner tension that is the focus of this chapter. We are men whose personal drive is high voltage. We are out to succeed. But we are also members of a brotherhood in which men are concerned with the success of the other fellow. These two facts often come in conflict. We are compelled to compete with our brothers. You and I cannot both have the key pulpit in our area, and if I am to get it then I must root you out. You might call our situation the battle of the brothers. Or it might be described the way one writer pictured an international congress of prime ministers, foreign secretaries, and ambassadors. He wrote, "With the assembly collected, and the great men face to face, it is an orchestra of first violins." Someone else expressed it in a more touching manner. He says, "We are like porcupines. We get together to get warm and then stick each other."

Once during our vacation we stopped by the side of the road in Oregon's Cascade Mountains to have our lunch. Although we had planned to eat in the woods, the mosquitoes soon drove us into our small house trailer for protection. A good many of the little pests followed us in, however, and our children busied themselves killing them. When one of my boys had disposed of a large mosquito that had just had a full meal, he showed me his bloody finger, and said, "Daddy, what's that?" "Blood," I answered. "Where did it come from?" he queried. "Out of you," I said. "That's what he gets when he bites you." With that he shook the remains of the late mosquito from his hand and said, "I'm not going to kill any more of those. They are my blood brothers."

It is not uncommon for your brother to be the very one who digs into you. A husband and wife who love one another may yet be locked in a power struggle with a strong sense of competition with each other. Joseph's brothers were competing with him for position, and yet, in spite of their efforts to dispose of him, were not without their love for him. Much of the drama of Jacob's life centers around the fact that he was compelled to compete with his brother, for whom he felt a deep affection. This same problem showed up even among the disciples, when James and John sought to root out the others as they requested of Jesus, "Grant us to sit, one at your right hand and one at your left, in your glory." No one could doubt the fact that the disciples were devoted to each other; but neither is there room to doubt that they were in competition with each other.

In the Methodist ministry, the sense of competition is most acute at certain readily recognized times: when key appointments are still under consideration at the Annual Conference, when General Conference balloting is going on, and when a Jurisdictional Conference is electing a Bishop. But it doesn't stop there. At the organizational meetings of the General Boards at the beginning of each quadrennium, the scramble for influential positions and membership on the key committees is evident. I am not familiar with the organizational structure of the other denominations, but my friends in their churches tell me that, in terms of the basic problem we are discussing, they differ not at all from the Methodists.

In all denominations, the way in which a man assigned to a church often seems compelled to compete with his predecessor by telling what bad shape he found the records in, or how many people were glad to see the change, is embarrassing. And even denominational executives, after they have been elected and presumably have reached the top rung of the ladder, are not free to enjoy the spiritual fellowship of a ministry untarnished by personal ambition and the drive to stand at the top. They vie with one another for key committee assignments and membership on principal boards; intense jealousies are sometimes found among their wives, who insist on their prerogatives; they are often overconscious of the popularity other church leaders enjoy and they pull strings to gain additional advantages. Yet through it all they contribute their share to making the ministry a great brotherhood.

Now if we are to handle this inner tension brought about by the interplay of brotherhood and competition, we must look squarely at a number of facts.

First, anyone with a sensitive Christian conscience is uncomfortable with the thought that he is much concerned with his own advancement. If he is honest with himself, he has to admit that he is pleased when he is singled out for a special honor, and he experiences an unmistakable satisfaction when he is advanced in rank. And, conversely, he nourishes a few resentments when he sees the other fellow given the job he thinks should have come to him, and he experiences a twinge of envy when he sees those whom he judges to be no more worthy or capable than he managing somehow to land in a lovelier parsonage or a more beautiful church. But while he has these feelings, his Christian conscience prevents his being comfortable with them.

This watchful conscience, building a fire under his personal ambition every time he starts to enjoy it, causes him to behave in strange ways. For one thing, it makes him strive hard to give a satisfactory explanation of the advancements he does accept. "I didn't really think I was the one for this position," he will say, lying with every word. "So-and-so would have done a better job. But the Bishop insisted I take it." Another favorite way of easing the temporary dizziness a fellow feels when he has just moved a few steps up the ladder is to say, "I really hadn't expected to move at this time, but this was too good to pass up."

These and other similar comments are never so much a description of the facts as they are evidences of a skirmish. They show that inside the man who is speaking a battle is going on in which his ambitious self is trying to subdue a temporarily excited conscience, and he is eager to keep the valued fellowship intact, even though he has shifted his position in it.

Another evidence of this battle is to be found in the unkind things that men sometimes say about those who have advanced beyond them. The importance of these remarks is not in their relative proximity to the truth, but in the fact that they are simply what has come to the surface to show that, below, a Christian conscience is fighting with the injured pride of a fellow who watched his contemporary pass him by.

For some reason, the Christian conscience, and the drive to get ahead of the other fellow, don't seem to fit happily together. Jesus had little to say in praise of the fellow at the top of the heap. It was the one that went to the foot of the table that he moved to the head; it was the one who accepted the role of the servant who he said was the greatest; it was the man who became like a child who would come into life's riches; it was the meek who would inherit the earth; it was the persecuted whose reward would be great. Least, last, and lost were favorite words of his.

No wonder the Christian minister is disturbed by his own restless drive to be somebody important. It doesn't seem to square with his religious faith. Must he be caught forever in this conflict between his conscience and his desire, so that if he satisfies his desire and forges ahead he must soothe his conscience with all manner of fabricated explanations; but if he remains humble and stands back, he must battle the resentments that a wounded ambition have left him? No, the Christian minister is not faced with that kind of a dilemma. He has another choice, and that brings me to the second fact that we must face.

Ambition is not a sin. Much of our best work is done through a drive to achieve a higher position. Ambition, like sex, or science, or political power, is good or bad according to its use. As a matter of fact, you kill something very important in a person when you destroy his ambition. It is that drive to excel, to go farther than anyone else has gone, to do a better job than has previously been accomplished that has brought about progress. That's the way mountains have been conquered, new lands have been won, science has grown, and great governments have been established.

Obviously, therefore, if a minister suppresses his feelings of ambition until he becomes satisfied to serve "wherever the Bishop wants to appoint him," he has been tampering with the spark of progress and has written himself off as lacking the drive that makes great ministers. To suppress the desire to get promoted is no better than to give it free reign. Some of the most unpleasant people in the ministry are those in whom a strong desire to get ahead has been suppressed. Some of them have become bitter, others merely dull.

In handling feelings of ambition, the Christian faith counsels directed expression rather than suppression. When the two disciples applied for a promotion, Jesus didn't say, "You shouldn't have such ambitions, it isn't Christian." Rather, he said they were trying to get what they wanted in the wrong way. "Whoever would be great among you," he said, accepting the fact that they had the desire to rate a high position among their fellows, "must be your servant."

I remember once hearing an expert on religious education talk about handling energetic intermediate youngsters. In speaking about ways to manage their restlessness, she counseled, "Never say to intermediates, 'Don't wiggle.' But say, 'Wiggle this way.' " The energy is there and must be expressed. It is the function of the leader to guide it into wholesome avenues of expression.

Jesus was dealing with the disciples in much this same way. He didn't say, "It's wrong to have these feelings of ambition." Rather, he said, "Express your ambitions this way." If I have a drive to be somebody important. I'll only frustrate myself by attacking the matter directly and reaching for the top positions. I can satisfy the drive only as I become the servant.

It is when I take my place at the foot of the table that I am invited to step into the place of honor. It is the fellow who humbles himself who is exalted. That is why the word "minister" is a more satisfactory designation of our vocation than "pastor." Pastor suggests a superior relationship in which one assumes the role of the shepherd of the sheep, a presumptuous role for any human being to take toward his fellows, even if he is the parson and they the laymen. But minister is much more satisfactory; it means "servant," one who ministers. And it doesn't mean the servant to one's congregation, but to Almighty God. Here is room for all the ambition a man has: to serve God aright.

The third fact we must face is that variations in status and large differences in size of churches and salaries do affect the way we feel toward each other. The man in a struggling rural church may call the minister in the wealthy suburban parish by his first name, but don't let that fool you. He doesn't feel on a par with him, as brothers should. Similarly, no one is deceived for long by the brave assertion of the newly elected Bishop, "Lay off that 'Bishop' stuff. Our relationship has not changed." Such statements belong in the category of famous last words. A great deal has changed. Never again will the newly elected Bishop be one of the boys in the same sense that he was before. With a suddenness he himself had not anticipated he is thrust into a new and highly dynamic social setting, the College of Bishops, a fellowship from which his former friends are excluded. Although he assures his former buddies he will welcome their criticisms, he soon comes to question their judgment, and they are not long in learning that their friendship with him has assumed new dimensions. As time goes on, fewer and fewer of them venture to call him by his first name.

Within this brotherhood we call the ministry are different groupings and clear-cut classifications. I am not at the moment arguing the question of whether this is good or bad, or if it is inevitable, but merely stating it as a fact that we may as well recognize.

One result of this fact is the loneliness that ministers often complain of. Too often, when they most need the fellowship of the brotherhood, they feel so great a gap between themselves and the persons who may be near them geographically as to render a real interchange of affectionate good will a questionable venture. The fellow in the little church feels that the man in the big pulpit doesn't have time for him—and he may be right about it. Also he finds it hard to be completely natural with his denominational supervisor. Although most men are eager for every opportunity to be in the company of leading churchmen, they often become so strained and unnatural in their presence as to find themselves making silly remarks and innocuous observations.

In the meantime, top denominational executives and their wives also complain of loneliness. Always in the public eye, they must constantly guard what they say and the way they say it. The more distinguished assignment a man has, the more vulnerable he becomes.

I'm not sure what should be done about these facts, except to recognize them. I did discuss the question the other day with a missionary on furlough. I told him that it seemed to me there were fewer jealousies and less unhealthy competition among missionaries than among ministers in this country. He assured me that human nature is the same the world over, and that these factors are to be found in the mission field as well as at home. He did agree, however, that the fellowship among the missionaries seemed to be a more genuine one, and the struggle for status much less apparent. He suggested that this might well be due to the fact that most of them received the same salary, no matter what position they held or how long they had been on the field.

The next fact we should note is that the man who is promoted is not necessarily the one who deserves it. Some men do get the breaks while others, more capable, are forced to step aside as they pass by. We like to feel that virtue is rewarded in this life as well as in the next, and I think that to a large degree the more capable men do wind up in the top positions. Nevertheless, this church of ours is made up of human beings who are subject to error, and we have all seen men who didn't deserve it awarded an honorary degree, men who couldn't handle power thrust into positions of top denominational or interdenominational leadership, and fellows whose charm exceeded their capacity to produce catapulted into the pulpit that deserved a sturdier ministry than it got.

If one accepts this state of affairs as a fact of life, much as he accepts the weather, he may be saved from the awful wrenching of personality that accompanies the disease of resentment. It helps to concentrate on doing a good job in one's own station and not to presume to be the judge of who really should have been called where, and at what salary.

A fifth fact we should consider is that to be overlooked has its effect on one's personality. I may not be made of the sturdiest stuff, but I know that I never do so poorly as when what talents I have seem to go unrecognized, and I never do so well as when my services are in demand. As a matter of fact, I think I am quite a different personality under the two situations. There is no question but that there is something about success that breeds more success, and there is something about failure that tends to spiral downward.

While it is true that too much success can go to a man's head and cause his ruin, and the necessity to deal with failure and disappointment can be the making of him, it is also true that a few promotions can be the stimulus to encourage a sensitive fellow to do better than he ever dreamed was possible, while persistently watching others advanced beyond him may be discouraging enough to make him morose, insecure in his leadership, and defensive. I am sure there are men among us, who have been checked off by themselves and others as mediocre, for whom it might have been another story if, early in their ministry, they had received the encouragement of promotion; and I am sure there are others, who are now enjoying the security of status and the well-being of the personality whose talents are recognized, who might be bitter and defeated except that at a critical moment in their career they got a break. In this I do not envy the men who are in charge of ministerial assignments. It's an awful thing to feel one holds the destinies of human personalities in his hands, and one could ruin himself by lying awake nights worrying about what he had done to a man or his family by one move or another. But, recognizing the ever-present possibility of making personality-shaking mistakes, he has no choice but to carry out his assigned task as prayerfully and as devotedly as possible.

When Stanley became Prime Minister of England, and undertook to form his government, he told the Queen he wished to entrust the leadership of the House of Commons to Disraeli. Interrupting him, the Queen said, "I do not approve of Mr. Disraeli. I do not approve of his conduct to Sir Robert Peel, and Sir Robert's death does not tend to lessen that feeling." Stanley responded by saying, "Madam, Mr. Disraeli has had to make his position, and men who make their positions will say and do things which are not necessary to those for whom positions are provided." It should be added that when in later years Disraeli himself became Prime Minister, he became the most beloved of all who had served the Queen.

Many men in the ministry have had a parallel experience. Their true worth unrecognized, they are forced to say and do things not necessary to those whose road to success has been smoother. Often this has made the best men unattractive to the ecclesiastical hierarchy. We need to understand the fellow who, all his life, has had to fight for his position as opposed to the one who has moved easily from promotion to promotion, or the one who, landing in a situation where growth is inevitable, has remained astride his horse, refusing invitations to move to a church where results are harder to come by.

The next and related fact we ought to note is that to be promoted gives a special kind of self-confidence. I once heard a marriage counselor tell of an unmarried woman who had stated that there was a self-confidence a married woman possessed, just because she was married, that a single woman could not know. It was the confidence that comes from the knowledge that someone had picked her out from among all the possibilities as the one he wanted to marry.

This same truth carries over into the ministry. I think I shall never get over the wonder of seeing men burst into bloom following a promotion. We have all observed it when some retiring and relatively little-known minister is elevated to a position of prominence. With the new confidence that comes with the added status and responsibility, he reveals a quality of leadership and a depth of Christian understanding we had never suspected was there. Men often become more at ease when they are promoted. No longer fighting within themselves in that battle of striving for promotion, they use their energies to do the job at hand. Again, Disraeli is a good example of what we are saying. When he finally became Prime Minister, and the Queen accepted him with delight, he felt his status was assured. His biographer says of him, "The security of victory brought a kind of relaxation. Never had the man been so completely natural. At last he knew that he would be accepted for what he was. He loosened his grip on himself. His wit was less harsh, less sarcastic." To be promoted does give a special kind of self-confidence.

The next fact I want to register is that we all need to pay more attention to the deliberate cultivation of deep friendship with our brothers. We have emphasized the importance of the work of denominational executives in arranging suitable promotions for men. But that does not absolve the rest of us of responsibility. In his little book *I Believe*, Bishop Kennedy writes:

Katherine Hathaway was a lifelong cripple who with God's help built a rich and full life. In *The Little Locksmith*, the story of her life, Miss Hathaway tells of a college friend who always drew out the best in people. This friend's talent was to see in a timid person "something rare and important and to make other people see it too—above all, to make the person in question feel it and be it." She would hold this person, who had been so colorless, up in a certain light, "like a collector showing a rare piece, and the person, in her hands, would suddenly receive a value and importance which made the people who watched the transformation wonder how they could have been so blind as never to have seen it before."[1]

I have felt that happen to me in the hands of kindly brother ministers, and I hope I may be granted the grace to extend a similar ministry to others.

When Arthur Compton, after delivering an address on the subject of the atomic bomb, was asked whether or not there was any defense against it, he paused a moment, and then replied, "Yes, there is." Then he added, "There is one defense —good will." Something like that is the answer we might give to those who would ask if there is any answer to the problem of our tensions brought on by our striving for position. The answer is good will, genuine concern for our fellows. Paul put it well in his letter to the Ephesians when he wrote, "Accept life with humility and patience, making allowances for each other because you love each other" (Phillips). And again, in his letter to the Corinthians, he wrote, "Love has good manners and does not pursue selfish advantage. It is not touchy. It does not compile statistics of evil or gloat over the wickedness of other people. On the contrary, it is glad with all good men when Truth prevails" (Phillips). And in writing to the Romans he again emphasizes the personal devotion to each other that can hold the brotherhood together. He writes,

"Let us have no imitation Christian love. Let us have a genuine break with evil and a real devotion to good. Let us have real affection for one another as between brothers, and a willingness to let the other man have the credit. Let us not allow slackness to spoil our work and let us keep the fires of the spirit burning, as we do our work for God" (Phillips).

We don't pay enough real attention to each other; we are too busy for that. But the almost lost art of friendship through letter writing and unhurried hours together should be revived among us. There is too much saying we ought to get together some time but never making it. The negative element of competition never flourishes among men who are genuinely and deeply fond of each other. As they wrestle with common problems and are devoted to a common task they are bound closer together.

In his book *Power to Manage Yourself*, Harold Walker writes of a boyhood foursome who called themselves "The Four Horsemen." He says:

We worked and played together, fought together, and got into trouble together. On one occasion we were close to blows. Harsh words had been uttered and threats voiced while we were on our way home from school after an annoying brush with education through the day. We were on the brink of a real battle when we were hailed by an old gentleman sitting at the wheel of a two-cylinder Maxwell automobile. He said his auto simply would not run and would we push him to the combination livery stable and garage three blocks away?

We put our shoulders to the car and slowly moved it foot by foot. We huffed and puffed and slapped each other on the back. Laughter punctuated our pushing, and in due time we reached the garage where the combination blacksmith-mechanic helped us push the offensive automobile inside. The job was done! Our quarrel was done, too, and "The Four Horsemen" were one again. Our difference, born in "ego," had been dissolved in our devotion to a common task to which we gave our strength. We lost sight of ourselves pushing.[2]

In the last analysis that's where our egos are dissolved, too—in our devotion to a common task. Not just any task. But *the* task—the only task worth our life's devotion—service of the King of Kings.

IV

THE PASTORAL ADMINISTRATOR

❖ ❖ ❖

Disraeli, even in his old age, was popular with the ladies. He was a favorite of the Queen, and most other women found him intriguing. Once at a dinner party of dancing girls, the question was asked, "Which would you like to marry, Gladstone or Disraeli?" All but one of the girls chose Disraeli. When the others booed her, she said, "Wait a minute! I'd like to marry Gladstone and get Disraeli to run away with me, just to see Gladstone's face!"

The story is not without its application to the ministry. When I was in seminary, most of the men wanted to be great preachers. The administrative responsibility they would accept because a certain amount of it went along with the job, but their real calling, they explained, was to preach. I have watched the men in the years since, and some have become great preachers, but most of them have done far more in the field of administration. They married the preacher but ran away with the administrator.

In his book *The New Class*, Milovan Djilas characterizes the various Communist leaders who have developed the philosophy and practice of communism, especially in Russia. Speaking of Stalin, he says he "looked neither far ahead nor far behind. He had seated himself at the head of the new power which was being born—the new class, the political bureaucracy, and bureaucratism—and became its leader and organizer. He did not preach—he made decisions." I suppose

Stalin is the extreme example of a preacher turned administrator, but all of us must be on our guard lest it be said of us: "He did not preach—he made decisions."

That administrative duties dominate most ministers' lives there can be little doubt. Move among our brother pastors at a typical ministerial meeting, asking each one you greet, "Well, how are things going?" and see what kinds of answers you get. One will tell you how his building is proceeding; another will give you his total Easter attendance; some enterprising brother will tell you of the survey he is making in his parish; others will speak of finance campaigns and new parsonages, or regional meetings and denominational boards. Few, indeed, will mention the books they are reading, the theological problems they are seeking to untangle, or the difficulties they are encountering in their endeavor to interpret the Christian gospel to their people through preaching. Partly this is due to the fact that buildings and finance campaigns and programs are tangible, and easy to latch onto in answer to so general a question as "How are things going?" But in a larger measure, men answer in these terms because they are thinking in these terms, and they don't know what else to say. One is reminded, in this connection, of the pilot who was asked by a passenger, "How are we doing?" He answered, "We're lost, but we're making good time."

Approach it from another angle. Try to arrange a time for a meeting with a group of ministers and see what the conflicts are. You can name them in advance: denominational board meetings, weddings, ministers' breakfasts, meetings of the trustees, executive committee luncheons, and the like. Any of these "previous appointments" are recognized as bona fide bases for adjusting the suggested date; no one will quarrel with them. But let a man say frankly, "I'm sorry, I can't come to the meeting: I bought a fine book yesterday, and I'm going to stay home and read it," and he will be considered unco-operative, an intellectual snob, or just odd.

When you stand back and look at the average minister answering the telephone every time it rings, opening his mail and spending too much time reading promotional material and the parish papers from other churches, clearing a few matters with a committee chairman, running to the printer to check proof, opening and closing church doors, adjusting thermostats, and arranging chairs, you are reminded of the way a novelist described the little town of Ophelia in Missouri. He said, "The drama of life there has no acts, only intermissions."

Now let me pause to make two things clear. First the church needs good administrators, and these remarks are not intended to belittle the importance of that fact. The larger and more complicated an institution becomes, the more urgent is the need for men whose administrative skills are superb. And second, the typical minister as we have described him above is not only failing to be a good preacher; he isn't a good administrator either.

Here then is the crux of our problem and our reason for including it in this book. As we observed in the preceding chapter, most of us have an intense drive—even compulsion—to succeed. But we aren't sure which path leads to success, so we try to travel all roads at once—a perfect formula for the achievement of mediocrity.

One evening, just before his bedtime, my small son was granted ten more minutes of play. There were two things he wanted to do, but he was required to choose between them. He could play ball with his daddy, or go over to the neighbors to play with a small friend. Although it was a difficult decision to make, he chose to go to the neighbors. When his ten minutes were up he came home crying. "What's the matter?" I asked. He answered, "I thought I wanted to play with Charles, but as soon as the ten minutes were up, I decided I wanted to play ball with you."

The dilemma we ministers face is not altogether unlike that.

Put in its crudest form, our problem is how to achieve status in the eyes of our laymen, among our fellow ministers, and in the world at large. One day we think the way to accomplish it is through great preaching, but the next day we are convinced that no minister will rate professionally who isn't doing some spectacular things in the field of evangelism or church building. Sometimes we conclude that if we are going to accomplish anything in our local parish, we have got to stick to it and work like beavers; then we see some dim star rising to prominence through a sacrificial piece of work in his conference, diocese, or presbytery, and we get to wondering if we will never get a chance to demonstrate our particular value until we become a wheel in the denominational machine. We go along for a time, doing a fairly decent job in our limited way, and then attend a meeting where we hear success stories about the techniques this man used to bring two hundred new members into his church last year, the clever ideas another man employed to put over a record-smashing finance drive, and the way someone else built a great church by emphasizing the importance of missions. In addition someone tells how important it is for the minister to be a good counselor, and someone else reports the number of house calls he has made, assuring us that pastoral visits are needed today more than ever before. Then someone hot on homiletics announces that the job of the minister is to preach and all other things are secondary. The minister, having come to the conference to get a lift, goes away guilt-laden and depressed. What Paul said to the Corinthians might be said to him: "It seems that your church meetings do you more harm than good" (Phillips). He recognizes the legitimacy of all the claims that have been made by the various speakers; he knows that of course he ought to be doing a great job in each separate field; he fancies that other men are succeeding in all these things while he is not. This makes for a severe frustration. Sometimes he drops what he had well started, and begins something new because he thinks this is what he must do if he is to ring the bell. Sometimes, with a great burst of energy, he starts forward moves on a dozen fronts, only to see them die of malnutrition when his energy is spent, rendering him helpless to bring to to each the continued creativity it demands. Sometimes, when frustration is most acute, he just becomes worn out thinking about it, and wearily plods on, fighting sickness and discouragement as he does what circumstances force him to do, but he has energy for little more.

A recent editorial in the *Christian Century* was written after the editor had reviewed the annual reports of the various denominations. He said that two words stood out in sharp relief: "New records," and commented that "a statistical report without that heartening aside is becoming more and more of a rarity." Each denomination made its claim to the achievement. For example, "The Methodist Church received a record $25,779,279 for home and foreign missions in the fiscal year ending May 31, 1957, disbursing for missions a record $25,206,494. And Methodist Church schools attained a record enrollment of 7,058,427." We are all caught in this record-crazy age and, besides contributing our share to the total for the denomination, we knock ourselves out to achieve a few new records of our own. But these goals are not achieved without a good many hours on the telephone, in committee meetings, and poring over budgets and plans.

In the meantime, people who are really more eager to find the Christian answers to life's perplexing problems than to be members of the largest church school in the area wait wistfully for the minister to speak the word that will touch their need. Some do not wait. When a man's body was pulled from Lake Michigan with a bulletin from a Presbyterian church in his pocket, the ministers confessed that it was a sober reflection to ask if they had nothing to say that Sunday to a man who was despondent.

This is the tension under which we live and serve, the inner conflict which we must resolve if we are not to break down. How can we administer the work of our church, co-operate with the denominational program, call on our people, do an effective job of counseling, keep up on our reading, maintain an example of happy home life, bring our church to the end of the year with a few new records, and preach like an inspired prophet?

Of course the obvious answer is that we can't. Nevertheless, the pressure is on us to do so, and our problem is how to handle the pressure. I am going to comment briefly on two inadequate solutions people employ in facing this dilemma and then suggest a few steps toward finding a solution that is real.

One inadequate solution is to become a dictator. When one has much to do, and little time in which to do it, he soon learns that dictatorial methods save time. If he applies them now and then, he also learns that a sizable group of people like being told what to do and how to do it. A man of decision gives them confidence and the lost chance to have things done their way is a small price to pay for the security that comes from having a leader who obviously knows where he is going. Once a minister discovers this fact, his dictatorial tendencies are likely to increase steadily. He may be a benevolent and even a fatherly despot, or he may become blunt and quite unconcerned about the feelings of others, but in either event he has tasted the wine of power and rather likes what it does to him. A disproportionate number of denominational executives and ministers of large churches have learned to accomplish twice as much as the next fellow by the simple device of giving orders and making it sufficiently uncomfortable for anyone who challenges them to discourage active opposition or prolonged debate.

One Christmas we received a mimeographed letter from friends who were serving in the technical assistance program in India. The wife, who wrote the letter, told of their plans to use their Christmas vacation, including Christmas itself, for traveling. She described the exciting trip they were going to take, and then added, "One slight difficulty—Charles told the children we would vote on whether or not to go, and the majority would win. They voted a strong, solid NO—but he wasn't worried, for he figured he could win them over in time. He spent several days talking it up, but the block held, and now he has the problem of changing that vote to yes." Then she added, "Those of you who know Charles well, know that somehow we'll go!"

This describes a good many ministers. They go through the motions of democracy, but no alert person can be in their church for long without realizing who calls the plays.

But dictatorial methods are ugly whether they are employed by Khrushchev, the Pope, or some Protestant preacher. Lord John Russell used to say, "When I am asked if such or such a nation is fit to be free, I ask in return, is any man fit to be a despot?" And a public relations man in our own generation, examining the moral implications of the increased ability of men in his profession to form public opinion, said, "One of the fundamental considerations involved here is the right to manipulate human personality."

We preachers must face up to that problem too. We are not necessarily most successful when we have the largest number of people functioning under the smoothest organizational machinery. If we have built our kingdom through permitting or encouraging adoration of ourselves, or through smooth administrative manipulation or direct commands, we are denying Protestantism's basic democracy and rendering little service to the Christian faith.

A second inadequate solution to the conflicting pressures that encircle the minister is the appeal to pity. Some men in our profession consume their energy eliciting the tender concern for their welfare that a good many people, looking for someone to feel sorry for, are all too ready to give. I am seldom impressed, when visiting a church, if everyone from the minister's wife and secretary to the Sunday-school teachers and church hostesses say of their beloved pastor, "Dr. So-and-So is a wonderful person, but he is so overworked. The people just won't let him alone. He's going to kill himself on this job." And of course that is exactly what he's trying to do. If he can keep himself sufficiently worn out to make a convincing bid for pity, he can stave off any criticism an unfeeling parishioner might be tempted to lay at his door because of his failure to do a better job. And he can ease his own conscience besides. How could he be expected to be a great preacher when "the people make such demands" on his time and strength?

But we have no right to live disorderly, undisciplined lives and then blame our deficiency onto our laymen. If we are overworked it is because we want it that way, unless, indeed, we are ready to admit we are helpless pawns in the hands of the people, and have no power over our own lives.

The appeal to pity does no good for us personally, and certainly is harmful to the profession. Not enough men are going into the ministry. In 1958 the Methodist Church received 979 new ministers. We lost 1,307 through death, retirement, location, or withdrawal. The net loss was 328. No doubt other denominations show similar losses. Enrollment in theological seminaries is slow to increase, and ministerial recruitment has become a concern of major importance among church leaders. There may be many reasons why we are failing to recruit an adequate number of young men for the ministry, but one of them is the poor impression a good many of us have made on the young men who come to know us. They don't want to enter a profession where they will be pitied for being overworked and underpaid.

If a minister is not to be permitted to resolve his tension by exercising his authority or by inviting pity, how is he to handle the problem?

The first thing he should do is to take a good look at the total job we call the ministry. Most of us are so immersed in it we do not see it clearly. Frustration dims our sight. We are acutely conscious that we have too much to do, but the vision of exactly what it is that demands our attention is blurred. We speak of being "swamped" or "loaded" or "behind the eight ball." These are vague exclamations that confess frustration but do not delineate responsibility.

Of course, a certain amount of frustration is desirable. When Edward Steichen was a young man struggling for recognition as an artist, he concluded he was a failure, and one day, in the studio of Rodin in Paris, broke down and wept. The great sculptor, however, put his arms around the boy's shoulders and said, "That is the test of the true artist, always being dissatisfied, always doubting one's own ability." Those words were destined to be a guide and a comfort to him throughout his career. When his remarkable showing of pictures marked a milestone in photography and drew great crowds throughout this country and abroad, someone suggested to Steichen that this success must be a source of great satisfaction. He replied, "Satisfaction! Who can ever be satisfied?"

It is one thing to feel a healthy frustration because of failure to live up to the noblest in one's profession, or to reach the goals one has set for himself. A minister who is satisfied with the work he is doing is an egotist and a bore. But it is quite another thing to be frustrated through lack of a clear-cut understanding of what one's profession does require of him, or the absence of self-imposed goals.

Not only at the beginning of our career, but repeatedly thereafter, each of us should analyze the job. Perhaps we can't do it all, but at least we have an obligation to know what it is we can't do all of. We need to face up to what a great sermon really is, and at what price it is preached. We need to understand what pastoral care at its best really consists of, and by what means a "man of God" can orient the people of his parish to eternal verities. We need to be realistic about the administrative work that must be done in a church of any size, and especially a large one. And we need to understand the scope of the educational program that comes under our general oversight. Not until we understand as well as feel the magnitude of the job we are dealing with can we find a way to fit into it in such a manner as to be strengthened by our labor.

The second step is to clarify our own responsibility. Since we cannot do everything that comes within the ministerial calling, and it would be foolish to try, we have a responsibility to discover exactly what we can and will do.

Every man has his own genius and should capitalize on it. If a man has the intense feeling for life, the clarity of thought, and the persuasiveness of speech that are prerequisites to great preaching, he is guilty of a special kind of homicide when he sacrifices the preacher in him for the sake of getting statistical reports in accurately and on time. On the other hand, he is robbing the church of distinguished leadership if, in his conviction that the preaching ministry is paramount, he struggles through a lifetime of mediocre pulpit work when his real talent is to set some tangled church machinery in order, creating the setting in which some other man can do the talking.

All the successful ministers are not of one type. This is something that those of us who like to identify the ministry with some particular approach find hard to accept, but it is true. Preaching has always been my emphasis and I used to think that no man could build a great church without it. But I saw a poor preacher build a great church through his sheer love of people and his dogged ringing of doorbells, and I had to rethink my position. Some men have a genius for Christian education and others for worship. There are also those whose particular bent is to maintain a surprisingly satisfactory balance between all phases of the ministerial office. They seldom excel in any one of them, but they often emerge with a substantial congregation, a solid organization, and a thoroughly progressive church enterprise.

Ordinarily, however, a man needs to decide which of the many roles in the ministry is to be his dominant one, and give his best to it. One of the psychology courses I took in college was taught by an elderly woman who had the rare gift of true wisdom. Talking about the frustrations so many students experienced in their all-out drive to get top grades in everything, she pleaded for more common sense. "Pick out the courses that are most important to you," she advised the class, "and work for A's in those. Get what you can out of the other courses, but don't set your sights for more than B's or C's." Her advice is as applicable to the ministry as to the work of the college student. Let each man choose that which is important to him, and do his A work in that field. Other matters can take the raveled edges of his time and energy. When one deliberately organizes his life this way, he relieves his conscience from the burden of not doing perfect work in all areas.

Looked at in this way, the ministry is a rare opportunity in this day of narrowly defined vocational fields. It offers a selection of emphases, and consequently a chance for individual genius to flower. This is a fact to which we should give greater emphasis. Paul considered it important. He said, "Men have different gifts, but it is the same Spirit Who gives them. There are different ways of serving God, but it is the same Lord Who is served. God works through different men in different ways, but it is the same God Who achieves His purposes through them all. Each man is given his gift by the Spirit that he may make the most of it" (Phillips).

We must recognize quite frankly that the current trend is away from such individuality. This has been brought startlingly to our attention in such books as Vance Packard's *The Hidden Persuaders*, William H. Whyte, Jr.'s *The Organization Man*, and David Riesman's *The Lonely Crowd*. Vance

Packard refers to "the trend in American society to the other-directed man—the man who more and more belonged to groups and played on teams," and points out that "people who coalesce into groups, as any general knows, are easier to guide, control, cope with, and herd." He calls attention to the fact that the team concept has become an important aid to "big business, big labor, and big government," which currently dominate the American scene, and quotes as typical the statement of Defense Secretary Charles Wilson, who, when some of his leading subordinates expressed their own feelings, growled, "Anyone who doesn't play on the team and sticks his head up may find himself in a dangerous spot."

In this same vein, William H. Whyte, Jr., stated in an article in *Fortune* magazine, "A very curious thing has been taking place in this country almost without our knowing it. In a country where individualism—independence and self-reliance—was the watchword for three centuries the view is now coming to be accepted that the individual himself has no meaning except as a member of a group."

My nine-year-old daughter is inclined to accept this point of view. One day she heard me mention a sermon entitled "Conformed or Transformed." "Daddy," she asked, "what does 'conformed' mean?" I explained it meant being like other people, wearing the same style clothes, using the same figures of speech, nurturing the same prejudices. In contrast, I pointed out that being transformed, as I had used it in the sermon, meant to be inspired by a higher goal than just to be like other people. She listened attentively and then said, casually, "I think I'm conformed. But I like it that way. It's more fun."

Because it is "in" this modern world, and to a surprising degree "of" this modern world, the church reflects these trends. Among us, as elsewhere, individuality is not always encouraged. Challenged to play a team game, ministers who are not suited for it are swept with the tide into participation in programs which, though valuable for some, are a waste of time for others. In this day of the organization man and other-directed people the church must emphasize individual freedom and the truth that the Kingdom of God is within each individual quite as much as where "two or three are gathered together." The modern church has done its share to popularize the current fad for togetherness. It has been out in the lead in promoting such worthy endeavors as group therapy and group dynamics, but let us not lose sight of the fact that the Christian religion is not primarily concerned with the individual in relation to the group, but the individual in relation to God. It is still true that the most prophetic utterances come from God-inspired individuals and not from group reports. "Godly," "inspired," "prophetic," "devoted" are all adjectives more properly applied to a person than to a conference.

Al Capp often reveals unusual insight into what is going on in the world, sharing it with us through Li'l Abner. Recently, Li'l Abner's son, Honest Abe, demanded, "Ah wants mah own private comb!" "Whut's wrong wif th' Yokum *Fambly* comb?" asked Li'l Abner, pointing to the almost toothless comb that hung from a nail on the wall. Then he added, "Usin' this comb gives our fambly 'togetherness'—th' *fambly whut combs together stays together!*"

Our challenge in the church is to create a climate in which each individual can realize his own potential. If we are to work as a team, let it not be for the accomplishment of some stereotyped program that a committee fancies will be good for all of us, but for the fulfillment of the individual genius of each minister. But preferably, let's not be a team at all. This is a concept that belongs to the secular world, not the Christian. Christianity is a brotherhood, and that is a different matter. The ethics of the football field are not the ethics of the Christian Church, but the ethics of the home are. The football field has no room for the individual who doesn't play a team game; the home embraces the whole family. The purpose of the football game is to get the ball over the goal; the purpose of the family is to discover the unique attributes of each personality and develop them in the service of God.

It is time to rethink the ministry along these lines and encourage each man, not to be a good *Methodist,* or *Baptist,* or *Episcopalian,* but to be a good *minister* working in his chosen denomination. Let him not pattern his ministry after that of anyone else, nor seek to make it conform to some fancied notion of what the organization expects of him. But let his ministry be different from what anyone else has ever worked out. The one consistent thing about the great prophets and preachers of history was their uniqueness. They became great by doing what God wanted *them* to do. It is almost safe to say that the uniqueness of a ministry is the badge of its authenticity. St. Paul stands in a class by himself. There was only one Luther. John Wesley had to do it his own way. How effective would Fosdick have been if he had not resisted the limitations that many Presbyterians or Baptists of his day would have imposed upon him? Would Henry Crane have been the power he has been in Christendom if he had stayed home to run his church according to traditional concepts of the ministerial task or under slavish adherence to denominational directives? These men recognized what their unique power was, and insisted on following their individual bent.

Don't think it was easy. Many successful preachers have found out that it is hard. Throughout their ministries they have been criticized for their failure to conform. People want their ministers to fit into familiar patterns of behavior. They are more comfortable with them that way. But when such ministers have the courage to resist the forces that make for conformity, and to follow their own inner direction, they can be expected to bring first-rate leadership to the church.

Paul once said frankly, "Christ did not send me to see how

many I could baptise, but to proclaim the Gospel" (Phillips). With no less forthrightness, each minister should determine what God has called him to do and, laying other things aside, declare his right to do it. This does not excuse him from being co-operative, nor nullify his responsibility to the church as an institution. Rather, it gives him a sound basis for co-operation and increases his chance of rendering the church significant service.

Our next step, after we have surveyed the entire ministerial field and determined our particular role in it, is to inform others, especially the members of our congregation, of our decision. That is what the early apostles did. Confronted with criticism because they were not administering the work of the church to the satisfaction of all, they said boldly, "It is not right that we should give up preaching the word of God to serve tables. Therefore, brethren, pick out from among you seven men of good repute, full of the Spirit and of wisdom, whom we may appoint to this duty. But we will devote ourselves to prayer and to the ministry of the word."

The problem was that there were certain administrative duties the apostles were about to have forced onto them, robbing them of the chance to do what they felt they were uniquely called upon to do. Now it is interesting to observe the developments. They had been criticized and were on the defensive. But instead of saying, "Thank you for the suggestion, we'll see what we can do," thus adding one more job to an already overloaded schedule, they came out with a clear statement of just what their responsibility was, and how this matter could be referred to someone else. And do you know how the people took it? This is what the record reports: "And what they said pleased the whole multitude, and they chose Stephen, a man full of faith and of the Holy Spirit, and Philip, and Prochorus, and Nicanor, and Timon, and Parmenas, and Nicolaus, a proselyte of Antioch. These they set before the apostles, and they prayed and laid their hands upon them."

When the apostles made it perfectly clear where they stood, their conviction was respected, the criticism stopped, and, what is more, the people picked up the work they were complaining to the apostles about and did it themselves.

People today are not so different from what they were then. They are not above criticizing their minister for his failure to live up to their expectations. But for the most part they are reasonable individuals and they wish him well. Once they come to understand and appreciate his role as he sees it, they can be depended upon to encourage him in his work, and put their own shoulder to the wheel to accomplish what he doesn't do.

Although we blame them for expecting so much of us, the problem really centers more in ourselves than in our people. Most of us give them the idea that we think we should be good preachers, pastors, teachers, counselors, administrators all in one. They are gracious enough to respect the job analysis we have led them to believe we have set for ourselves. They often think we are a little stupid to try to do so much; but if we are willing to do it, they are willing to expect it of us. The fact is, however, that the day we come before our board with a well-outlined and clearly defined description of the church's task and our part in it, they respond like a lost army that has found its general. They want us to have something we emphasize and do especially well; it gives them something to admire in their minister. They want us to leave clearly specified areas of the church's work to them; they are in this business because they believe in it and want a job to do. They want us to challenge them with the need for additional staff members to carry certain areas of the load. They like to feel their church is growing, and they are smart enough to know that two full-time men can do a great deal more than one can.

But here is the rub: many men are not willing to let go of

any part of the ministerial responsibility. They like being the hub around whom the wheel revolves, and while they complain about the load, they aren't eager to shift some of the weight to another axle. It gives them a feeling of importance, albeit a false one, to be consulted before anything is done, to be called on for prayers at all meetings, and to be looked to as the only one who is qualified to counsel the disturbed or call on the sick. They frankly enjoy doing all these things and don't want to give any of them up. As long as it is evident they expect to be called on for everything, they will be.

I enjoy leading singing and recreation, but it is not what I consider my principal ministerial responsibility. These talents, if I can so dignify them, lay hidden during my first few months in my present church. Then, at a large party in our home, I directed the games and led the singing. The people had found a new facet to their minister's personality! At once I started receiving requests to lead the recreation for this group and direct the singing for that one. But it was not for this that I came to the Kingdom, and I was not about to drain off my energies in this direction even though it promised to be the source of a satisfying popularity. Firmly but kindly I turned down most of these invitations. So far, I have heard not one word of criticism for this. On the contrary, since I had previously outlined clearly what I considered my role to be at this church, they were quick to say, "We understand. You have a more important job to do."

When people understand what we conceive our job to be, and when it is evident we work hard to do the job as we have described it, they respect us and do not expect us to do the impossible.

It needs to be said, further, that even after a minister has made up his mind not to try to do everything, and when both he and his people have come to understand just what part of the ministerial task he does give his major attention to, he will still very likely be overworked, at least by present-day standards. He narrows his field of concentrated labor, not so he will have more free time, but so he can render a more significant service. He will still put in more hours than 90 per cent of his laymen, and will accomplish more in a well-organized week than some people do in a month. But the work will be easier because much of the tension will be off. Nevertheless, he must continue to find times to get away from it all to find the repose that nothing but separation from the daily task can give. Eleanor Roosevelt, who carries a heavy schedule herself, has good advice. She says, "Sometimes it is extremely good for you to forget that there is anything that needs to be done, and to do some particular thing that you want to do. Every human being needs a certain amount of time in which he can be peaceful. Peace may take the form of exercise or reading or any congenial occupation; but the one thing which must not be connected with it is a sense of obligation to do some particular thing at some particular time." Similarly, Clovis Chappel, in a lecture to ministers, said, "the most religious thing a tired man can do is to rest. Every man who really works ought to rest one day in the week. Every man ought to take a vacation at least once a year." Even Jesus recognized the necessity now and then to "go apart and rest a while."

If we come to understand what this job we call the ministry really is, determine our own part in it, clarify our role to our people, and in addition get the rest, recreation, and quiet that we need, the tensions that accumulate around the multiple role of the ministry should be somewhat relieved.

V

SPIRITUAL PREACHING AND MATERIAL COMFORT

❖ ❖ ❖

Hal Boyle reports that he is in bad standing at one home where a small boy asked him about heaven. He says, "I did my best to explain to him all about this place where I hope some day to get my mail. I answered all his questions with the latest information I have." Later, however, the boy's father reproached Boyle. "What ideas are you putting in my son's head anyway?" he asked. "He has informed his mother he never wants to go to heaven because it doesn't have an escalator. He says he would rather go to a department store."

The boy's reaction should not surprise us. Most people find the secular more appealing than the religious. That's why theaters draw more people than churches, and shopping consumes more time than praying. In spite of the current "popularity" of religion, most moderns aren't much interested in Christianity. They are interested in business, politics, sports, and scandal. The daily papers are an index to that. They print what people want to read. You don't find much about religion on the front page unless a preacher has robbed the church treasury, or run off with another man's wife.

This is not a criticism of the newspapers. It is not a criticism of anybody. It is just a description of things as they are. In most cities of the world, unless the church does something unchurchly, religion is largely unnoticed.

This is more than simple lack of interest. Much that passes

for indifference is really hostility. Not everyone who fails to put in his appearance at church on Sunday morning is merely careless about his religious duties. There is something more than the urge to sleep, or play golf, or work in the garden that accounts for the absence of many. They just don't like church. They do not enjoy the company of "church folks." They do not like what we say nor the way we say it. They are opposed to our morals, which they think are stuffy and narrow. They dislike our stands on social issues, and demand that we stay out of politics. They don't like our hymns and they resent the reminder that God expects them to be better persons than they are.

There is nothing unusual about this. The church has done its work in a hostile society since Jesus warned that "men shall revile you and persecute you and shall say all manner of evil against you falsely."

Sometimes the opposition has been brutal: Christians have been driven from the city, burned at the stake, fed to the lions, locked in concentration camps. And sometimes the opposition has been subtle, as expressed by the sophisticate who walks by the church without even noticing that it is there. But whether overt or oblique, the opposition is present and it is real.

Nevertheless, the evangelistic urge is strong, and in spite of every discouragement we continue our efforts to Christianize the pagan world. If we revise our time schedule and surrender our hope to win the world for Christ in this generation, we still instigate the encounter of "Christ and culture" and seek through the intellectual writings of great theologians and the "two-by-two" visits of drafted laymen to teach an errant society to recognize its Master's voice and heel at the church's command. Inspired by the Biblical injunction to become "fishers of men," fired by statistics about the number of children in our communities who are not in Sunday school, and stimulated by our natural evangelistic zeal, we ministers annually enroll our laymen in a concentrated effort to bring the wanderer home.

But there is a problem. We are a minority with a majority complex. Ninety-nine to one, the story of the Good Shepherd has it. We are the outcasts trying desperately to be the status group. Assuring all who come within the sound of our voice (and there aren't many) that their hearts are lonely until they rest in God, we add few converts. Meanwhile, our own hearts ache to be fully embraced by the circles of secularism from which we have separated ourselves by a self-imposed exile.

When one minister's wife sought treatment from a psychiatrist for her depression, he convinced her that her problem was her moralistic separation from her fellow human beings. The cure was to take up smoking and cocktails to restore her sense of unity with mankind.

So conversion takes place in reverse. The twentieth-century American, caught up in the dynamics of free enterprise with its engineering, business administration, politics, and Hollywood entertainment, finds little in Christianity to entice him. He can take it or leave it alone and usually leaves it alone. The minister, however, finds he cannot be so casual about the secularist's world. Its smart furnishings are attractive to him and its sophistication is at once an annoyance and an enticement. He is captivated by the glamor of it, and a willing prisoner of its comforts.

And that's a switch. The lump has changed the leaven more than the leaven has changed the lump. Those who would turn the world upside down have got upset themselves. The great evangelizers have been evangelized. While the Christian clergy have been cheering their little bands on to win the world, the world has quietly won them.

Most Christian ministers are materialists. They are secular in everything but their talk, and sometimes even their pulpits are indistinguishable from the lecture platform. Take a typical man of the world and compare him with a man of the cloth. He buys the finest car his income will allow. So does the preacher. He moves from an inferior to a better neighborhood, from a humble to a more pretentious home. So does the preacher. He buys all the comforts he can afford, enthuses over passing fads, and puts his faith in vitamin pills, antibiotics, and psychiatrists. The preacher is inclined to do the same.

Evidence of clerical materialism is not hard to find. Let's begin with salaries. On the average they are not exceptionally large, but we talk about them too much. We dig out figures to prove they haven't kept pace with the cost of living, and we enumerate the professional expenses we must pay out of our own pockets. Most of us accept without much question the generally held notion that ministers are underpaid and could be making twice the salary if they were in some other work. Meantime comparatively little is said about the fact they are getting their house and sometimes their utilities free, and that they are granted a nice car allowance for which their church requires no accounting.

The men fuss around a good deal about whether the salary should come to them in one bundle or be broken into various expense items to save on income tax. Not the least of these considerations is how it will look in the denominational journal. Some have also been known to go slow in pushing for much needed additional staff for fear the added expense would adversely affect their own salary.

All in all, we have little of the disdain for this world's goods that was the mark of the circuit riders who were lucky if they got three meals a day, or the deaconesses who pledged to serve on a subsistence level.

Take a look at parsonages. They aren't often the finest homes in the community, but the roof over our heads is usually a large one and often shelters furnishings that are both comfortable and attractive. The minimum requirements for new parsonages in the California-Nevada Conference of the Methodist Church as of June, 1958, included three bedrooms and a study, two baths, a two-car garage, central heating, built-in kitchen stove, dishwasher and garbage disposal unit, and air conditioning and insulation where these seem advisable. With patience, parsonage committees can be depended upon to bring their ministers' residences up to standard, although some of the more eager brethren hasten the day of fulfillment by designating their own church contribution for parsonage furnishings. "Where your treasure is, there will your heart be also."

No doubt many parsonages are inadequate. Few of them, however, would seem humble to Kagawa, Muriel Lester, or Jane Addams, nor to Him who had nowhere to lay His head.

Ministers drive fine cars, and turn them in with surprising frequency. It's supposed to be cheaper that way. They boast of the good deals they make. Some seminary graduates arrive at their first appointment in expensive station wagons, drive them hard, and trade them in for new ones in a year or two. It's "necessary" in their profession. But I should like someone to tell me why it was necessary for a minister, appointed to a small church in the Alaska Mission, to ship in a Buick when everything in town was within easy walking distance and it was impossible to drive a car more than fifteen miles on either side of the town. He is not to be criticized personally for this. He was merely acting in accordance with popular standards.

Perhaps some light can be shed on ministerial cars from a passage in The Hidden Persuaders. "After psychiatric probing a Midwestern ad agency concluded that a major appeal of buying a shiny new and more powerful car every couple of years is that 'it gives him [the buyer] a renewed sense of power and reassures him of his own masculinity, an emotional need which his old car fails to deliver.'"

The minister's materialism is not confined to salary, home,

and car. He looks at his church through the same eyes and is likely to know more about the house of God than the power of God. In recent years we have become preoccupied with buildings. When I went to my present church many ministers extended their sympathy because of the old building I inherited. It is out of date, and scarcely what is so neatly described these days as "functional." But every Sunday it houses as fine a group of consecrated laymen as you are likely to find anywhere. None of my ministerial friends thought to mention this.

Motivated by the conviction that we must build modern facilities to attract children and youth, we have gone on a building binge. The myth is abroad that if bulldozers and lumber trucks haven't been seen near your church lately, you just aren't preaching the gospel.

I am in favor of building. Modern facilities do make a difference. But for the sake of our souls we ministers should pause now and then to reflect upon the effectiveness of One whose church was as wide as the earth and whose pulpit was the spot where He stood when He spoke. We should give serious thought to the words of the critic who asserts that never have the churches "been materially more powerful and spiritually less effective" than today. James Robinson puts it plainly. He says, "Sometimes, with all due reverence for the symbolism and the tradition and the holiness of sacred places like churches, I think it might be a good thing for churches per se to be destroyed, thus dispersing God's messengers to the four corners of the cities in which they live. This might force them to build their Holy places, not by famous architects' plans and specifications, but by the strength of the message they can deliver on hilltops, street corners, wind-swept avenues, subway stations, railway terminals and bus terminals. Here, of all places in the world, one would surely find those whom God is waiting to heal."[1]

Now we must not overemphasize the materialism of the

minister or we shall miss the point of this chapter. There is another side to the preacher. He believes in the things of the spirit.

Some time ago an interesting advertisement was run in *The New York Times*. It began by telling how the Vice-President of the United States got his start in politics by answering an ad calling for "a young man to be a candidate for Congress."

From this beginning, the writer of the *Times* ad continued, "I cite this interesting bit of recent history because I also have the problem of finding the right man for an important job. My associates tell me I'll never get my man through the paper, because he won't be reading any help-wanted ads . . . he doesn't have to! Well, I haven't flushed him out any other way, and if an ad in the paper could turn up a man good enough to be Vice-President of our country, maybe another ad can turn up one good enough to be EXECUTIVE ASSISTANT TO THE PRESIDENT of an international corporation that is steaming toward the two-hundred-million-dollar-a-year mark, with the throttle wide open and a clear track ahead."

The ad proceeds to give some details. Salary is hinted at. "Fifty Thousand Dollars a year won't buy the man I want . . . I know that . . . because he's already making at least $40,000 a year, and another ten thousand or so will not be THE inducement. So I'm ready to cross that bridge when we get to it . . . with compensation geared to the facts of life."

More is said about the qualities this man must have, and then the ad is brought to a close with this: "P.S.—Religion is of no consequence . . . the only religion considered will be a consecration to effort and achievement."

This is true secularism. It nourishes few ulcers since the tension between the material and the spiritual is broken. A thoroughgoing materialist enjoys peace of mind because he has released religion from its mooring. He is not tormented by the yearning to sail the sea and fight its storms in search of a better land. He remains securely on shore to enjoy the fruits of a materialistic society, free from the annoyance of a nagging conscience.

But this grace is not granted the Christian minister. Although he builds his home on the shore, his ship waits for him in the harbor. He likes his comfortable life, but he cannot close his ears to the sound of the waves or his eyes to the beckoning horizon. He is a stranger here. Heaven is his home.

So the preacher mounts his pulpit to tell his people not to lay up "treasures on earth where moth and rust corrupt and where thieves break through and steal," but to invest in spiritual values. He admonishes them to seek first the Kingdom of Heaven and God's righteousness and let the material things take care of themselves. He states that "a man's life does not consist in the abundance of his possessions" and warns of the catastrophe that will befall the man "who lays up treasure for himself, and is not rich toward God."

But the message does not always ring true. We American preachers of the twentieth century are in the curious position of preaching a gospel of the cross from the comforts of a couch. We declare the superiority of the spiritual while enjoying a life absorbed in the material. Against this background a gospel of sacrifice sounds hollow. Any sensitive minister is aware of this, and is less comfortable with his conscience than with his car. There is something basically unnerving about going out to a steak dinner after telling a congregation that for the price of a milk shake you can feed a Korean orphan for a week. Donald K. Faris visualizes the hungry of the world in terms of a line starting from your front door and extending over continent and ocean, 25,000 miles around the world and back to your front door. But it does not end there. Passing your home a second time, it encircles the globe again and again—twenty-five times in all. And no one in the line is adequately fed. All are hungry. The line is growing at a rate of twenty miles a day. Every two years enough additional hungry people have been added to the population to make a new circle around the earth. As it stands now, it would take you three and a half years, traveling ten hours a day at fifty miles an hour, to travel the length of the line of the hungry people of the world, and by the time you got to the end it would have grown so much longer that it would take you several more months to catch up with it. A famine strikes in China and millions die, their bodies littering the roadside, food for dogs—and humans. A priest leaves his comfortable parish to give himself to the 3,000 boys and girls without known parents, making their home in the dry riverbed that snakes its way through the stinking slums of Santiago, Chile. A Navy doctor gives himself unstintingly to the sick and wounded refugees from North Vietnam. At least one victim was so horribly mutilated by Communist brutality that the doctor had to step outside the tent and vomit before he could treat the wounds.

These stories can be multiplied a thousand times as the drama of human suffering is enacted daily on every continent. The preacher knows these stories, and he tells them to his people on Sunday, and modestly accepts the raise they vote him at the Wednesday-night board meeting. He calls on his congregation to sacrifice for Christ and His Church while he looks for a ministerial assignment with a maximum of personal advantage. Having begun our careers with commendable idealism, many of us wind up in middle life thinking, if not saying, "I'll go where you want me to go, dear Lord, if I can be guaranteed the comforts I am accustomed to."

We are not happy with this state of mind, but what can we do about it? Some men simply close their eyes to it.

At our house we often play games at the dinner table. It is a way of focusing the children's energies on a single project and maintaining a reasonable degree of mealtime order. On New Year's Day it occurred to me to deviate from our usual games, which were beginning to wear thin anyway, and make some New Year's resolutions. I explained to the children that they were to think of something they did last year they were sorry for, and of a way they would try to improve on things this year. The game started with enthusiasm. Jerry was going to quit tearing his nails. Doug was going to be happier around the house. Lois Ann planned to help her mother more. When it came four-year-old Tommy's turn, he looked up at me and said solemnly, "I pass." When it comes to life's annoying problems many of us would like to skip that turn.

It is surprising how many ministers meet this tension between their own material comfort and their need to identify themselves with the suffering people of the world by pretending it isn't a problem. They rationalize, and come up with all kinds of justifications for maintaining a high personal standard of living and enjoying it. They say a minister has to live on essentially the same level as the people to whom he ministers. They maintain that powerful automobiles and stereophonic sound are a part of our generation, just as oxcarts and tomtoms belonged to an earlier one, and that it is foolish not to avail yourself of the best any age has to offer. They speak of the sacrificial lives they lead, working long hours and submitting to the emotional drain of counseling, and insist that they have earned the right to these comforts; they deserve them. They compare themselves with those who are more extravagant than they, and comment on their own really humble way of living.

No doubt there are elements of truth in all of these arguments, but they are more a reflection of our state of mind than an objective reflection of the facts. Our thinking is like a salad bowl in which our ideas are mixed with our emotions before they are served. No thought emerges from any of us except after it has been flavored by our fears, anxieties, hopes, and ambitions. The conviction that God wants us to have all these modern comforts is strongly conditioned by the fact that we want to have them. It is easy for a child to tell his mother,

"Daddy thinks it will be all right" when that isn't exactly what Daddy said.

A very different state of mind is revealed in the conclusions of Eugene Debs, who, imprisoned for conscience' sake, wrote: "While there is a lower class I am in it, While there is a criminal element I am of it; While there is a soul in prison, I am not free."[2]

This was not mere rhetoric; it was a way of life. Reflected in his words can be seen the state of his emotions.

Some men accept all the comforts our capitalistic society has to offer, and soothe their consciences by criticizing the system that produced them. Others, who seem more honest if less prophetic, boldly equate the Kingdom of God with a system of free enterprise. In his book *The New Class*, Milovan Djilas says, "Under Stalin the party became a mass of ideologically disinterested men, who . . . were wholehearted and unanimous in the defense of a system that assured them unquestionable privileges." The same can be said about some preachers. Paul described them in his letter to the Romans when he wrote, "These men deliberately forfeited the Truth of God and accepted a Lie, paying homage and giving service to the creature instead of to the Creator" (Phillips). Charles Templeton has put it straight. He says, "We need to remember this; we are not to come to terms with this world, we are to change it! We are not to adjust to it for it is out of joint. It is upside down and needs to be turned right side up. There is a false peace of mind which is only a temporary alleviation of the real problem of the alienation of our life from God."

In Maxwell Anderson's play *Winterset*, Mio, a troubled youth, victim of some of the crueler things society does to its children, is talking with a girl whom he met near the bridge outside her home. He says to her, "Tell them when you get inside where it's warm, and you love each other, and mother comes to kiss her darling, tell them to hang on to it while they can, believe while they can it's a warm, safe world, and

Jesus finds his lambs and carries them in his bosom.—I've seen some lambs that Jesus missed."

At summer youth conferences we sometimes go to bed at night to the sound of taps: "All is well; safely rest; God is nigh." But sooner or later the Christian minister has to surrender the illusion that "it's a warm, safe world," and leave his fireside in search of the lambs that Jesus missed.

It is said of the disciples that "they forsook all" and followed Him. But it is possible to go too far in this direction too. There is no evidence that you alleviate poverty by becoming impoverished or that you reform a social system by becoming subservient to those who have made it what it is. The absolutist position, whether it is the absolute acceptance of materialism or the absolute rejection of it, is untenable.

We come then to this: the answer to our dilemma is not evasion or a sell-out to materialism, nor yet a divorce from the time and place in which we live. Rather *it is a frank acceptance of the tension.*

It is too simple an answer to renounce the material in favor of the spiritual. Besides, the line between the material and the spiritual is an impossible one to draw. If a magnificently appointed church lifts the minds of worshipers to the throne of God, who is to say it is too expensive? And if a humble parishioner, who never had much of this world's goods, finds the lovely home of the minister—a home he helped to pay for—a restful refuge in time of trouble, could we say with any confidence that a shack with few conveniences would have served as well? One of the effects of Christianity in any land is that it tends to raise the standard of living. Can we accept the religion and reject its effects?

Yet the temptation to accept these effects—by-products, we might call them—as the goal is a constant threat. So we must live out our ministry, sustaining the tension between spiritual preaching and material comfort. Somewhere there may be a point of near balance which allows for a grateful acceptance of material blessings free from guilt feelings for their possession.

Meanwhile, it is impossible to set a satisfactory limit on material possessions. One man thinks it is wrong to own a Cadillac, so he buys a Ford. But another says the Ford is too expensive and gets a Volkswagen. The final test must be in the use to which one's possessions are put. The owner of the Cadillac who uses his car effectively in God's service is more justified in ownership than the one who, with a Volkswagen, uses his car only for his own selfish purposes.

Harry Emerson Fosdick had the right spirit. He knew that material advantages may be a curse or a blessing according to their use. Before he moved with his congregation to the new Riverside Church, he said this in one of his sermons:

You know it could be wicked for us to have that new church—wicked! Whether it is going to be wicked or not depends on what we do with it. We must justify the possession of that magnificent equipment by the service that comes out of it. If we do not, it will be wicked. . . .

Very frequently in these days people come to me and say, The new church will be wonderful. My friends, it is not settled yet whether or not the new church will be wonderful. That depends on what we do with it. If we should gather a selfish company there, though the walls bulged every Sunday with the congregations, that would not be wonderful. If we formed there a religious club, greatly enjoying themselves, though we trebled our membership the first year; that would not be wonderful. . . .

If all over the world, at home and abroad, wherever the Kingdom of God is hard bestead, the support of this church should be felt and, like an incoming tide, many an estuary of human need should feel its contribution flowing in, that would be wonderful. If young men and women coming to that church should have Isaiah's experience, seeing the Lord high and lifted up, his train filling the temple, and if they too should discover there their divine vocation—"Whom shall I send and who will go for us?"—and should answer, "Here am I; send me," that would be wonder-

ful. If wherever soldiers of the common good are fighting for a
more decent international life and a juster industry, they should
feel behind them the support of this church which, though associated in the public thought with prosperity and power, has
kept its conviction clear that a major part of Christianity is the
application of the principles of Jesus to the social life, and that
no industrial or international question is ever settled until it is
settled Christianly, that would be wonderful. And if in this city,
this glorious, wretched city, where so many live in houses that
human beings ought not to live in, where children play upon
streets that ought not to be the children's playground, where un-
employment haunts families like the fear of hell, and two weeks
in the country in the summertime is a paradise for a little child,
if we could lift some burdens and lighten some dark spots and
help to solve the problems of some communities, that would be
wonderful. If in that new temple we simply sit together in
heavenly places, that will not be wonderful, but if we also work
together in unheavenly places, that will be.[3]

It isn't just what you have, but what you do with what you
have that counts. The question for the minister is not simply
how lovely is his parsonage, but how well does he use it; not
how big is his church, but how much service does it render.

A man can be ruined by modern comforts if he gives his
soul to them, but he doesn't have to let that happen. Paul
said, "Don't let the world around you squeeze you into its
own mould, but let God re-mould your minds from within"
(Phillips). When that happens a man is emancipated from
materialism although he is in the midst of it. In the world,
he yet is not of the world.

During many of the years of his long life, Herbert Welch
has been a Methodist Bishop with the salary and expense account that go with the office. He has mingled with the world's
elite, and yet his ministry has not been caught in the tentacles
of materialism. The story of his life reads like the adventure of
St. Paul:

We have traveled by bicycle and motorcycle, auto and airplane, ricksha and chair carried on the shoulders of coolies, in a jolting Peking cart and on elephant back.

We have traveled on narrow-gauge railroads in Korea and wide-gauge railroads in Manchuria, and freight cars, and once, at least, on top of a car. This was all right until it began to rain.

Sometimes we have traveled under soldier guard in China because of the solicitude of magistrates.

We have come through sea storms and sand storms, through a typhoon in Japan and a hurricane in New England, and through a fire that destroyed our home.

We went through the great Japanese earthquake and through the Korean independence movement, which was rather more exciting, on the whole, than the earthquake.[4]

Because a man is amply cared for from a materialistic standpoint is no reason for him to rot on the vine. His very abundance can open new doors of service if he is determined that it shall be so.

Jesus said, "A man's real life is nothing to do with how much he possesses" (Phillips). But he condemned "the man who hoards things for himself and is not rich where God is concerned" (Phillips). Surely his counsel to his disciples is still the guiding star for the Christian minister: "Don't worry about life, wondering what you are going to eat. And stop bothering about what clothes you will need. Life is much more important than food, and the body more important than clothes. . . . You must not worry about getting food or drink, or live in a state of anxiety. The whole heathen world is busy about getting food and drink, and your Father knows well enough that you need such things. No, set your heart on His Kingdom and your food and drink will come as a matter of course" (Phillips).

VI

THE PROFESSIONAL FAMILY MAN

❖ ❖ ❖

One Easter Sunday the sermon I gave at the Sunrise Service was recorded to be broadcast later in the day. Being a modest sort of fellow, I tuned in to hear a good speech. Suddenly my two small sons, possibly attracted by the fact that the radio was louder than usual, came running into the room to see what was going on. "That man sounds like you, Daddy," the older one observed. "It is," I said. "Is that you?" asked the younger one, looking at me with amazement. "Yes," I assured him. "It is." Satisfied I was telling the truth, he asked, "Well when are you going to come home?"

I'm sure that neither he nor I realized how frequently this question would be asked at our house in the years to follow. Unuttered or expressed, it has a prominent place in the minds of most preacher's children. It seems to them that Dad is gone a lot.

A few years ago, when I was traveling in Europe, I received a letter from my wife in which she said that one of our boys had been quite homesick for his daddy. One night he prayed, "Dear God, please help us remember what our Daddy looks like." That's no joke. Most ministers, maintaining the highest ideals for wholesome Christian family life, sustain a perpetual fear that their children will grow up without seeing enough of them even to remember what they are like.

Of course ministers are not the only men who face this problem. Speaking of the executives, who have become so prominent a part of our culture, William H. Whyte writes, "Executives try to be dutiful husbands and parents, and they are well aware that their absorption in work means less time with their family even when they are physically with them. Younger executives in particular accuse themselves. They are not, they say, the fathers they should be and they often mention some long-term project they plan to do with their boy, like building a boat with him in the garage. But they add ruefully, they probably never will. 'I sort of look forward to the day my kids are grown up,' one sales manager said. 'Then I won't have to have such a guilty conscience about neglecting them.' "[1]

That most clergymen have a guilty conscience about neglecting their children there can be little doubt. When one group of ministers was trying to select a time for holding regular meetings, Monday seemed to be the day agreeable to the largest number. But one young man protested. "Monday is my day off," he said, "and the one chance I have to be with my family." He received quick support from the oldest man in the group. "I used to think the ministry required me to work seven days a week," he said. "But I want to bear my testimony that if I had my life to live over I would devote at least one day a week to my family." His conviction on the matter was obvious to everyone, but most of the group did not know that, as he spoke, he was thinking of his alcoholic son.

The problem is further complicated by the fact that even when a minister is home he is not free to give himself to the family as a good father should. He is with them in body but not in spirit, which is almost worse than not being there at all. It is humiliating to a little girl to relate the events of the day to a father who grunts indifferent responses, his mind on the agenda for the evening board meeting. And it is frustrating to a boy to have his dad start to help him with his algebra only to be called to the phone before they figure out the first equation. Often a phone call requires that the minister make another one to clear some detail, or that he go to his study for a few minutes to make some important notations. In the meantime the slighted son has to adjust as best he can to the secondary claim he has on his father's attention.

A good symbol for the ministry is a bell—not the one in the church tower calling the devout to worship, but the one that responds to the whirl of somebody's dial or to a finger on the button beside the front door. It is hard to escape it. Even when the minister dons his old clothes and heads for the garden, vowing that he won't answer the phone if it rings, he is scarcely a free man. Some neighbor will spot him just after he gets his garden tools assembled for action and will amble into his yard saying, "You are always so busy, I never want to bother you. But perhaps this will be a good time to ask you a question that has been on my mind."

At that moment the squeak of unoiled wheels and the clatter of little feet announce the arrival of the minister's little girl, who comes running around the corner of the house pulling her wagon and carrying her small rake, shouting with excitement, "I'm ready, Daddy. Where shall we work first?"

"Good girl!" commends daddy. "I'll be with you in a minute. Maybe you could get started raking the leaves under that tree."

"I don't want to bother you, Reverend, but it's my only chance to see you."

"That's all right. She'll have fun raking the leaves, and we can sit here where we can watch her. What is the question you wanted to ask?"

"Daddy, I'm getting a big pile already, see."

"Yes, dear, that's very nice. You're a big girl."

"What I wanted to talk with you about is our son. He's nine years old now and hasn't been baptized. We moved around so much when he was small that we just didn't have it taken care of. I don't think we ought to wait any longer, do you?"

"Daddy, I'm tired. When are you going to help?"

"I'll be there in a little bit. There are some big pretty leaves over on that side, why don't you rake those into a pile?"

"I don't want to rake. I want to work with you."

"What do you think, Reverend?"

"Daddy."

"How does your wife feel about it?"

"Daddy."

"She thinks it would be embarrassing to do it now, and says she would rather just wait and let Bill decide this for himself when he's a little older."

"Daddy! I want to talk with you!"

"Come and sit on my lap, dear. Mr. Moore and I are talking and you are interrupting. Be a good girl, and I'll help you with the leaves pretty soon."

"Oh, all right."

"Perhaps it would be better if I were to talk with you and Mrs. Moore together."

"I don't think that would work so well. She doesn't understand."

"Is it 'pretty soon' now, Daddy?"

"Not yet. Do you think it would work well for me to give you an opinion, and for you to deliver the message to your wife?"

"Come on, Daddy."

"Now that you put it that way, I guess I am approaching it a little oddly. But I just can't get anywhere with that woman. You know, Reverend, sometimes I think—"

"Daddy, you promised we were going to work in the garden."

"Yes, dear, I know. But Mr. Moore is asking me some questions and I want to help him if I can."

"I'm asking you questions, too, Daddy, but you don't help me."

"I will. Just be patient."

"I'm tired of being patient."

"What was it you were starting to say about Mrs. Moore?"

"Well, I hadn't planned to tell you this, but she's getting harder to live with all the time. Do you know what she did yesterday?"

At this point a small girl walks slowly away, and as the men continue their conversation her voice can be heard from around the house lackadaisically calling toward the wall of the house next door: "Judy! Judy! Can you come out and play?" And near the two men in the garden is an abandoned wagon, a pile of leaves, and a small rake.

The problem the minister faces is not a simple one. He really wants to work in the garden with his little girl and he thinks he should. In addition to the fact that his daughter needs this experience with her daddy, he needs the diversion and the exercise. Besides, to enable his church to maintain its self-respect, he feels a compulsion to get the parsonage yard into shape. But he also wants to talk with Mr. Moore, and as a good pastor he feels he should. The garden is a natural setting for their conversation, and he should take advantage of the fact that Mr. Moore is in a mood to talk about something he has kept to himself for a long time. If he should tell Mr. Moore to come back later, or to make an appointment through his secretary at the church office, he would very likely discourage his neighbor from talking with him at all.

The whole situation contributes mightily to the minister's inner tension. He is supposed to be the perfect father, and his home an example of Christian family life at its best. But he must often choose between being the kind of husband and father he would like to be and the kind of minister he would like to be. How can an effective minister be a good father and husband?

One certainty is that he must find a middle road. The answer does not lie with either extreme. The minister who is a married man has embarked on a double career, or, perhaps more accurately, a single career with two facets. But however you phrase it, he has a responsibility to both aspects of his life and neither is to be sacrificed at the altar of the other. This is not to say he must divide his energies and his affection and thereby weaken them. Rather, he must enlarge them and thereby strengthen them. The minister who takes his role of husband and father seriously is a better minister, and the father whose vocation is the Christian ministry has better than an average chance to leave his children a worthy heritage.

It follows, therefore, that the minister who expects his family to do all the adjusting whenever there is a conflict between his role as a pastor and his role as a father has the wrong idea. Neglect of his family does not contribute to his stature as a minister. Nevertheless, there are men who are so dominated by a drive to fulfill their ministerial obligations that their families consistently come out at the short end. Probably these preachers do not realize how desperately children want some attention from their father and how deep the hurt is when they are consistently pushed aside. One preacher's small son offered his father ten cents an hour to stay home and play with him!

This is not to say that the children do not understand when their father confronts a conflict and must ask to be excused from some activity they had planned together. Children are wiser than most adults suppose. Probably they understand the total situation better than their elders, and they are ready to excuse and forgive. But they also understand that when they are *always* asked to take second place, their own father doesn't really care much about them. He will protest any such assertion and will make some feeble effort to disprove it, but the children are right.

Some time ago Norman Cousins attracted a good deal of attention with his article in *The Saturday Review* about the Ravensbrueck Lapins, a group of Polish women who had been victims of Nazi medical experimentation in prisons during

World War II. He had traveled to Warsaw to talk with them and see if they would accept help similar to what was given to the Hiroshima Maidens who were brought to this country from Japan. Speaking to the women through an interpreter, he approached the subject with great care, but he didn't seem to win their confidence. They were slow to respond. Then Mrs. Frubowa, his interpreter, turned to him and said, "I am sorry to have to tell you this, but I am afraid that it may be of no use. These ladies have used up all their hope. I don't think they believe the offer of help is true."

The preacher's family that has been pushed aside too many times is in somewhat that same position. And when they have "used up all their hope," there is not much a man can do to regain their confidence.

No minister ever intended that it would turn out this way. He didn't make up his mind in advance that he would neglect his family. He just got caught in a situation he never fully understood and from which he seemed powerless to extricate himself. Another look at William H. Whyte, Jr.'s *Organization Man* may help to describe the situation. Whyte says of the young executives:

Common to these men is an average work week that runs between fifty and sixty hours. Typically, it would break down something like this: each weekday the executive will put in about 9½ hours in the Office. Four out of five weekdays he will work nights. One night he will be booked for business entertaining, another night he will probably spend at the office or in a protracted conference somewhere else.

On two of the other nights he goes home. But it's no sanctuary he retreats to; it's a branch office. While only a few go so far as to have a room equipped with dictating machines, calculators, and other appurtenances of their real life, most executives make a regular practice of doing the bulk of their business reading at home and some find it the best time to do their most serious business phone work. ("I do a lot of spot-checking by phone from home," one executive explained. "I have more time then, and besides most people have their guard down when you phone them at home.")

While corporations warn against such a work load as debilitating, in practice most of them seem to do everything they can to encourage the load. Executives we talked to were unanimous that their superiors approved highly of their putting in a fifty-hour week and liked the sixty- and sixty-five-hour week even better. In one company, the top executives have set up a pool of dictaphones to service executives who want to take them home, the better to do more night and week-end work.

In almost all companies the five-day week is pure fiction. Executives are quick to learn that if they drop around the office on Saturday to tidy things up a bit it won't be held against them in the slightest. Similarly, while the organization encourages executives to do extensive reading of business periodicals and trade journals—often by free subscriptions—few executives would dream of being caught reading them in the office. Such solitary contemplation during the office day, for some reason, is regarded by even the executive himself as a form of hooky.

Executives admit that they in turn impose exactly the same kind of pressure on their own subordinates. Some lean toward praising men pointedly for extra work, others prefer to set impossible goals or to use the eager beaver as a "rate-busting" example to others. "What it boils down to is this," one executive puts it, "you promote the guy who takes his problem home with him."[2]

Ministers operate under a similar pressure. There is always more to be done than can possibly be accomplished in any reasonable working day. So the minister gets to his study early, holds a meeting over the lunch table, gives a pep talk at an evening dinner, and hurries back to the office to get some letters finished and in the mail before midnight. Even if he has a free evening, he is likely to go back to the church to catch up on things, or bring the work home with him. Sitting at his desk, he tells himself, "I should spend more time with the family. Perhaps when this campaign is over I can work something out." At that moment the telephone rings, and in response to an inquiry he can be heard to say, "I can't possibly do it now, Mr. Anderson. I'm loaded down with this finance drive. But I'll have a little free time when this is over. Perhaps we could squeeze the meeting in then."

Other people with whom he works do not help the situation. His denominational executive paternalistically warns him he is working too hard and he mustn't neglect "those fine boys" of his, and reminds him his denominational survey reports are already a week late and of course he wouldn't want to be guilty of holding up the entire study. His best laymen commend him on his "wonderful family" and urge him to spend plenty of time with them while they are young, and mention that Mrs. "I'll-Get-My-Feelings-Hurt-If-I'm-Neglected" has been in bed for three days and a pastoral call ought not to be put off much longer. In the meantime he is aware of the fact that his brother ministers who work without ceasing receive the commendation of laity and church officials alike. So, blinding himself to his responsibilities as a father, he presses on toward the mark.

There are some ministers, however, who go to the other extreme. They demand their right to live a normal family life and set themselves like flint against encroachments on their privacy. They tell their people the parsonage is the minister's private residence, and in this regard is not different from any other home. They entertain few, if any, church groups, and discourage individuals from dropping in at odd hours. Any affairs at their home are strictly private parties with their own special friends.

Often a fetish is made out of the family. "We think it is so important for the minister's family to do things together," Mrs. Minister will say with a sanctimonious air that infers divine sanction for her scheme to confine her husband to her domain for at least one full day a week. Apart from a few noble exceptions in which husbands have instigated highly creative and worth-while family plans, most ministerial households that make a great point out of the fact that the family comes first are matriarchal. Some woman is feeling neglected or frustrated or resentful and has laid down the law to friend husband. Not infrequently, an exaggerated insistence upon the right of the family to have outings and family experiences of their own carries overtones of resentment toward the church and a lack of devotion to its mission.

Do not misunderstand me. I am a family man, and believe in family solidarity. But this doesn't blind me to the fact that in recent years family togetherness has been emphasized all out of proportion to its importance. The healthy family is supposed to play together and pray together and camp together and garden together, and attend cub-scout pack meetings together, and come to family-night church programs together. Having tried all of these things, in company with my wife and four children, I claim the authority of the practitioner, and I want to say that most of the things we have set out deliberately to do as a family have been a flop. Children are not enthusiastic about what well-meaning adults think would be a wonderful family experience, and if the program is geared for the youngsters, most adults find it insipid. When thrown together with other families, the children, instinctively grasping their opportunity, head for the woods or the most remote section of the building, while their harried parents, neither being with their children nor enjoying relaxed conversation with other adults, give way to an evening of strumming on tense nerves. I, for one, am grateful that artificially induced family togetherness is a fad that is passing. I believe in the kind of family unity that comes about naturally where a man and a woman and an assortment of children happen to love each other, where each is concerned with the welfare of all whether individually or in groups, and where none feels compelled to prove they are a happy family by boiling them all in the same kettle.

It is easy for a minister, feeling guilty about neglecting his children, to blunder into the child's life at a point where he is not particularly welcome. One minister friend of mine decided it was time to be a pal to his young son, so he borrowed a bicycle and said to the boy, "Come on, Larry, let's go for a ride on our bicycles." Larry said, "What for?"

A woman called out from a crowd Jesus was addressing, "Oh, what a blessing for a woman to have brought you into the world and nursed you!" Jesus replied, "Yes, but a far greater blessing to hear the word of God and obey it" (Phillips). That is the note we are striking here. Nobody questions the value of family life, but it should be seen in its proper perspective.

So far in this chapter we have endeavored to state the problem and describe two inadequate solutions. The problem is the tension a minister experiences between his loyalty to his church and his loyalty to his family. The inadequate solutions are absorption in church work to the neglect of the family and an artificial family togetherness. Now we are going to explore some solutions that show more promise.

The first is to recognize the unique thing a minister's home is, and learn to value and enjoy it for its very uniqueness. No matter how hard a minister and his wife try to make their home a private residence like that of their parishioners, they will never be 100 per cent successful. And even if they were, they would not likely be pleased with their achievement. The vocation of the ministry calls for a home that is different. Efforts to deny this lead only to frustration.

One day a friend said to my wife, "I wouldn't change places with you for anything. I couldn't stand to live in a goldfish bowl." She was a perceptive woman who understood at least one way in which the minister's home is different. People who can't accept the fishbowl life had better look elsewhere for a vocation.

Another unique factor in the minister's home is that the

whole family is involved in Daddy's work, and they must all move at a fast clip to keep up with it. Family and church responsibilities are intermingled. The minister helps his wife get the children off to school and, if he is home, tucks them in at night. She helps him with his church work, filling him in on details that only a woman can pick up, offers counsel, and assists with the organizational routine. If this unusual kind of family involvement in the work of the husband and father is accepted and not resisted, a good time is had by all. But if members of the household insist that a minister's home, like the houses in a new tract, should look like all the rest of the homes in the community, tension and heartbreak are likely to result.

Another way in which a minister's home is likely to be different is in the amount and the nature of the entertaining that is done there. Children of the manse have a far better opportunity than most youngsters to come to know all sorts of people from the simplest to the grandest. The world finds its way through the doors of the minister's home. Most parsonages entertain a share of oddities who arrive for weddings or counseling. One overnight guest in our home was a man spending his first night of freedom after five years' imprisonment. He was reunited with his mother at our place. People of different races and nationalities sit at our table and sleep in our beds, and our children learn to know and love them. There is an East German pastor they call Uncle George and a young member of a wealthy and influential Hindu family in India with whom they have a casual first-name relationship. A Peruvian student lived in our home, also one from Korea. Our children have met and come to know friends from such interesting places as Ghana, Yugoslavia, the Philippine Islands, and various countries of the Middle East. Whatever hardships they may suffer from the fate of being preacher's kids, they are receiving an orientation in the emerging world that few others their age can duplicate.

Recently we moved from a small college community where there were almost no non-Caucasian residents to a large metropolitan area where Negroes and Orientals were in abundance. We moved into a fine neighborhood of well-kept homes where within a radius of two blocks there are Negro, Japanese, Chinese, Greek, Italian, and Jewish families living. One of my sons has a Negro French teacher, and children of many different racial backgrounds are with them in school. Our children accepted all this as though it were the most natural thing in the world. They came home from school talking about their friends, never thinking to mention that they happened to be of a different race. We could only judge by their names, or by seeing them when they were brought to our house to play, that they were non-Caucasian. I was telling a friend about this, and she said, "I envy you. That's an advantage your children have over ours. We couldn't get our children accustomed to mingling with people of other races without developing it artificially. It hardly seems appropriate to go around asking, 'Does anybody know a Negro we could invite to our house so our children can learn to be natural around people of other races?' " Ministers' children do have a distinct advantage here because of the unique thing that a ministerial home is. I once heard Mrs. Eugenie A. Anderson, when she was Ambassador to Denmark, say that she developed her interest in the people and the affairs of the world through her experience of growing up in a Methodist parsonage. Members of parsonage families understand what she meant.

Children of the parsonage also learn to know people of significance in various walks of life, and learn to feel at home around them. However, they sometimes embarrass their less casually adjusted parents. One day when I introduced my son to a state senator, I asked, "Son, do you know what a senator is?" "Yes," he replied. "It's somebody like Joe McCarthy."

Another interesting incident occurred when Dr. Georgia Harkness, noted theologian, was a guest in our home. Shortly before, our young son's pet guinea pig had died. At first unable to soften his grief with promises of another one—"There aren't any guinea pigs as nice as Spotty"—we had finally met success by promising we would get him a mother guinea pig that was going to have babies. A neighbor helped out by giving him a cage to house the new animal when it arrived.

While Dr. Harkness and I were in the living room talking, and my wife, "being great with child" had stepped in from the kitchen and stood in the doorway sharing our conversation, Doug came into the room and, addressing our guest, said politely, "Dr. Harkness, would you like to come down to the basement to see the cage for my pregnant mother?"

Parsonage families that come to recognize what a unique thing the minister's home is, and to enjoy and value its very uniqueness, have gone a long way toward solving the problems of parsonage living.

Another way to deal with the tensions that sometimes arise from competition between home and church is to make sure that each member of the family has status in his own right. The minister's family are not content merely to share their father's time. They also want to share his status—or, perhaps better, develop a comparable status of their own. As proud as they may be of the man of the house, the minister's family needs something more than to bask in the light of reflected glory. It is not enough just to be the preacher's wife or son or daughter.

I learned this truth early in my married life. A few weeks following our marriage, as we were driving home from a week-long youth camp in the Redwoods I suddenly became aware of a faint sniffling beside me. A quick glance to my right confirmed my worst fears. My wife was crying. Having not the slightest idea what had brought on the tears, I was totally unprepared to meet the emergency. Her first response to my inquiry as to what the trouble was you can easily guess: "I don't know." That's a feminine come-on with which all husbands are familiar, and I led on with the usual awkward questions designed to uncover the problem. But she is good at analyzing things herself, and in a short time she came up with the conclusion that there was nothing wrong with her except that she was finding it hard to adjust from a setting in which she was a leader in her own right to one where she was just the wife of a leader.

Pauline Trueblood describes the situation forcefully. She writes: "It has been my privilege to converse with many wives in my travels with my husband. I am always on the fringes of every public occasion which we attend, meeting the other women who are also on the fringes. We all know what it is to have our husbands introduced, with the opportunity of making a reply, while we are introduced in a manner which assumes that we are unable to make any response at all. We rise and smile. Personally, I should rather be ignored. If I could say even a few words I should feel more like a human being."[3]

Children are not always capable of describing their difficulty as accurately as these women do, but the problem is just as real. They, too, want to be something more than stage hands to keep everything in order for daddy, or the setting in which the new preacher can be photographed as evidence he is a wholesome family man. They want to be somebody important themselves. Bishop Kennedy has illustrated this in a simple incident that occurred on shipboard. He writes:

On my way home from Honolulu I was sitting on the sun deck of the *Lurline* and talking with two bishops of the Methodist Church. Our eight-year-old niece was with us on the trip and she had found few companions aboard, since most children were in school. She sat beside me for as long as she could stand it, and then broke in brightly: "Would you like to hear a riddle?" Now frankly, that was the last thing I wanted to hear just then, for we were talking about a most interesting situation in the Church. Besides I had heard the kind of riddles she had picked up from her friends. But it came to me suddenly that here was a little girl who felt neglected and she was saying to me, "I'm here too. Let me into this circle. Do not ignore me. I'm important."[4]

This is the unvoiced cry of many parsonage children. At least part of the time they want the spotlight to focus on them.

The wise minister will recognize the need of the members of his family for status, and will see to it that their need is met. If the minister's wife has a flair for organization and finds personal fulfillment in directing the activities of a group, family life should be organized in such a way as to make it possible for her to exercise this kind of leadership. Of course, care should be exercised that she not take the reins of the church out of her husband's hands, and if there is a tendency in this direction she should find an outlet for her drive in organizational activity beyond the local church and in the community. Other wives will find the satisfaction they need in one of the arts, music, or interior decoration. They should be encouraged to develop these areas of their interest so that they may experience personal fulfillment and be something more than somebody's wife. Children, too, should be led into situations where they can take the spotlight. When one of the minister's children is in a school program or is leading a church activity, the minister himself should make every effort to be present and sit in admiration at the child's feet just as the youngsters are expected to sit quietly in church and listen to their father preach. Ministerial family tensions can be reduced when each member of the family is assured individual status.

Another way to keep the ministerial household on an even keel is to maintain a wholesome, spontaneous honesty. There is a good deal of pious self-righteousness in some parsonage homes. The problems discussed in Chapter I, "Condemned to Sin Piously," may apply to the whole family as well as to the minister himself. Feeling somewhat on the spot, they may try to appear to be something different from what they really are. There should be no attempt to cover up the fact that family devotions, so ideally pictured in the church movies and magazines, just didn't click at the parsonage or that the man who preaches such positive sermons on Sunday may slip into a black mood on Monday or lose his temper on Saturday. There is no reason to be ashamed of the fact that the minister's wife who is always so charming and efficient is not really able to carry a superhuman job with equanimity. Like other normal women, she sometimes nags at her husband and lashes out unnecessarily at her children. We are rapidly emerging into an era in which human beings are not in danger of losing their good name when their human frailty is revealed. It's a wholesome change, and the church ought to lead the way.

Another way to maintain a stable home is for the minister to keep counseling within bounds. In recent years a great deal of emphasis has been put on this phase of the ministerial office. Many men get more ego satisfaction out of sitting before the admiring eyes of one counselee after another than out of preaching. This field is important but overemphasized. Many preachers, inadequately trained as counselors, stumble into deeper waters than they can navigate. Counselees often uncover weaknesses in the counselor's own personality structure and his feet of clay give way. There have been lurid newspaper accounts of ministers who have brought humiliation and heartbreak to their families and embarrassment to their churches by sexual involvement with someone who came to them to seek counsel. But these well-publicized cases are, regrettably, only a fraction of those that actually take place. The total number, however, is still very small in comparison with the number of men in the ministry.

Counseling is an intimate relationship between two people, and it can get out of hand. Most preachers know this. That is one reason they set up standards for themselves as to the type and extent of counseling they will do. One of the most important things for a minister to learn is when a problem is out of his range. If the difficulty is not basically spiritual, but is an emotional or legal or medical problem, he should be quick to make the proper referral. Some men also safeguard their integrity and their home, as well as their time, by setting a maximum number of successive interviews they will give to anyone. One minister has four as his maximum. If the problem is not yielding by then, he refers the counselee to a more specialized counselor. Even the minister who has himself well in hand in these matters must remember that too much time given to too few counselees is unwise. Extensive counseling with one person may or may not be a strain on his own emotions, but there is always the chance it will be misunderstood by his congregation and a cause for doubt in the heart of his wife. A minister should discover what type of counseling he is capable of doing well and then keep himself disciplined to what he can handle. One able pastoral counselor says that it is more the job of the minister to create a therapeutic climate than to do counseling itself. Be that as it may, no minister has the right to endanger the wholesomeness of his own family life by too great an obsession with counseling.

Consider another key to ministerial family happiness. Things will run more smoothly around the parsonage if one lets his church know that he needs a home adequate for the job he is there to do and that he expects them to care for the parsonage and grounds just as they care for the church and its grounds. Ministers are notoriously poor gardeners and fix-it-yourself men. Possibly they went into the ministry because they couldn't do anything else, but it is more likely that they are poor at these things because they haven't the time to spend with them. It takes time and money to keep a beautiful garden and to see that each leaky faucet is fixed and every broken hinge replaced. It takes more time and money in a minister's home than in most other homes because the average parsonage is subject to much heavier use than the homes of most laymen. All wives know the frustration of wishing things around the house were fixed—a broken mirror replaced in the

bathroom, new treads put on the stair leading to the basement, the dishwasher put back into working order. They also
know what it means to them, if they have any pride in their
home, to see a well-kept lawn and colorful flowers around the
house. The minister's wife is no different from other women
in this regard, and she is as tempted to nag at her husband for
not taking care of these things. Of course, he wants them in
shape too, but he simply hasn't the time to do all of this and
still do what his church people have a right to expect him to
accomplish in the parish. Therefore, the care of the parsonage
and the parsonage garden should be the responsibility of the
church members. Most lay people would be pleasantly surprised at how much more effectively the parsonage would be
used for dinners, parties, committee meetings, and entertaining church dignitaries if they relieved the parsonage family of
these particular responsibilities. And the family would experience a new sense of release and joy.

Another key to happy parsonage life is for the minister to
take his family into his confidence in connection with church
matters so that they feel included in the interests that consume so much of the father's time. This single factor may
make the difference between children who grow up loving the
church and identifying themselves with it and those who grow
up to resent it and ultimately to leave it. When a second child
is to be born into a home, wise parents prepare the first child
by telling him, not that his mother is going to have a baby,
but that he is going to have a little brother or sister. He is led
to help his mother ready the nursery and comes to take pride
in donating his own crib because he is a "big boy" now and
will have a big bed all to himself. His parents encourage him
to talk about "our baby" and how "we" are going to take care
of him. When the baby comes, his big brother is given the
job of taking friends into the nursery to see him, or he may
even be the one selected to hold the infant so that admirers'
exclamations turn easily to him and he is not overlooked.

Thus a child comes to love the new baby and to identify himself with it. Failure to involve him in this manner, however, may easily lead to resentment and retaliatory actions toward the newcomer.

A child's relation to the church may be conditioned in this same manner. If he feels it is "our" church and is taken into confidence about what is going on, and is given an opportunity to fulfill his own personality needs in church-related activities, he will come to love the church and be identified with it. If he sees it as only a competitor, always standing between him and his parents or between him and what he wants to do, it will not be surprising if he rejects it.

Once when a lady took her two-year-old nephew, the son of a minister, for an outing, he ventured up the steps of the slide, but when he reached the top he lost his courage. He couldn't bring himself either to go forward down the slide or to back down the steps. He simply stood at the top and shouted. He didn't say, "I want to get down," or "I want my Mommy," or "I want to go home," as might have been expected. He shouted, "I want to go to church!" It is a blessed thing when the church is indistinguishable from other feelings of family security in the mind of a child.

It will also help to build a secure parsonage home if the minister recognizes that the true test of fatherhood is not in faithfully fulfilling routine fatherly "duties," but in that experience of reality the New Testament calls love. If I attend all the school programs, provide transportation for my youngsters, accompany them on scout camping trips, and help them with their studies, but don't really care about them, they will sense the low esteem in which they are held and their personalities will accommodate themselves as best they can to the damage done. On the other hand, if I truly am too busy for the multiplicity of little services to children that this generation has come to identify with being a good parent, but when I am with my children they know I love them deeply and care about what they are doing and what they are, they have the security of knowing they are loved, and there is no substitute for this. Some of the most inadequate fathers I know come through with flying colors when it comes to passing the cubscout test of what a good father is. But they have established no empathy with their child; they have led him into no worldwide interest or sympathetic understanding of other ethnic groups; they have done little to teach him how to think and love and worship.

Most ministers have libraries that are large and varied. What greater service can they render a child than to walk with him through this world of ideas, and talk with him about the concepts that have changed history and the dreams that have driven civilization forward? While, admittedly, books are not a substitute for physical exercise, and every father should find time to play with his children, I would far rather be known as a father who taught his child to use, to understand, and to respect a library than one who played football with his son on the corner lot. In the former instance I am being a father; in the latter I may well be rejecting my father role in favor of a return to childhood.

Just before his birthday one of my sons was talking with me about the expensive presents he would like to get. Then suddenly he turned to me and said, "Dad, I'd be glad to have a birthday without any presents at all if that would bring peace to the world." If he caught this idea from living in a parsonage, I am glad my son's dad is a preacher.

It is often difficult for the minister to shine in those things which this generation has popularized in a stereotype of fatherhood. But he has a multitude of opportunities not open to other persons. Besides the things already mentioned, he has a longer summer vacation than many men, and can spend an extended time in the summer getting close to the family as they travel, camp, or go to Disneyland together. Often he can arrange to take one of his children along when he travels to a

distant city, to keep a speaking engagement, or spends a week
at a youth conference. This intimate relation of Dad with one
child at a time builds a priceless relationship that will last
forever. I have personally found such trips very rewarding and
my children have been led through them into experiences that
have been both enjoyable and worth-while.

I would not want the preceding remarks to convey the
notion that a minister's life and his relations with his children
are devoid of physical play. Most ministers don't get enough
experiences of this kind.

One year while we were on vacation I spent a good deal
more time studying, planning and handling correspondence
than I did swimming and fishing. The most reckless thing I
did to prove I was on vacation was to stay away from church.
We planned our own services, however, which we held each
Sunday morning in the trees down by the lake. The children
were responsible for this, and did it all without any help from
me. My wife and I were the congregation. One Sunday morning they went through with their service as usual. The scripture
they took from Bowie's *Bible Stories for Boys and Girls*. The
prayer was from *Prayers for Girls*, and the offertory sentence
was from memory of hearing Dad. The sermon that day was a
passage selected from Lindbergh's *Spirit of St. Louis*. It didn't
seem too scriptural but it was more interesting than a good
many sermons I've heard and some I've preached. It was
about a priest whom Lindbergh was teaching to fly. The
priest was a reckless flyer, but he loved flying and happily took
to the air every chance he got. When he had finished reading
the story, my son closed the book, looked up at his audience,
and said gravely, "I don't know what moral Lindbergh had
in mind when he wrote this. But the moral I thought of was:
even a minister can have fun!"

I hope some of the sermons I preach reach their mark as
effectively as that one did.

One more way a minister's home may be strengthened is

by making sure that every member of the family has a chance for privacy. We have already mentioned the fishbowl nature of a parsonage. This makes it imperative that steps be taken to guarantee a degree of privacy to each member of the family. Each person needs a place to escape to when he feels the need to be alone.

George Hedley, the able chaplain at Mills College, insists that even the close union of marriage has no right to infringe too much upon a person's private life. One should still have "the right to read one's own mail, and to choose whether or not to share it." He should also maintain his "sacred right to privacy of thought and feeling, into which no other person, not even husband or wife, is entitled to pry."

Before concluding this chapter, I want to say a word to ministers' wives. In no other vocation is the role of the wife as crucial as it is in the ministry. The success or failure of a minister may well rest in his wife's hands.

A great deal is expected of a minister's wife. Like a nation's queen, she is thought of as symbolizing womanliness at its best. Church members want to look to her as an example of an attractive woman, a devoted wife, and a loving mother. They like to see her in her role as hostess, where she is most properly the "First Lady" of the church. She is expected to be an ideal homemaker and at the same time polished and charming in her public appearances. But she must do all this without a royal treasury from which to buy clothes and pay for household help.

In addition, some churches expect their minister's wife to take a major office in the woman's organization, teach a Sunday-school class, sing in the choir, and assume the chairmanship of a few committees. Where she has a particular ability and interest, and wants to assume one of these responsibilities, that is fine. But she should keep in mind that every official job she accepts beyond her distinctive role as minister's wife robs her of her chance to give her best to the one assignment that is hers alone. Others can sing, teach, and guide the work of a committee, but none can be elected to the role of minister's wife. What she fails to accomplish in this specialized area doesn't get done.

There is no simple formula for being a good minister's wife, but here are three suggestions that might help:

1. Seek to understand your husband. Many wives do not appreciate how much their husbands love their jobs and how deeply they are involved in them. "To the executive," writes William H. Whyte, Jr., "there is between work and the rest of his life a unity he can never fully explain, and least of all to his wife." The minister's wife needs to understand that at least part of the reason her husband is at home so little is that he loves his work so much. He assumes that she loves it too, and that is the reason he is mystified when she complains of being neglected.

There are many other things a minister's wife must understand. If her husband is going to make his mark in the ministry, he must buy and read books. She must realize that money that goes into reading matter is not necessarily selfishly spent even if it does mean she must postpone the purchase of a new hat another month. And she must remind herself that when her husband is quietly seated in a comfortable chair reading a good book while she is dressing the children, mopping the floor, and doing the dishes, he is not being lazy or inconsiderate, and he's not playing while she's working. He is on the job.

She also needs to understand that her husband must travel. As he becomes more and more involved in the work of his denomination, he will be called to meetings farther and farther from home. But, more than this, he needs to go abroad, to see at first hand what is happening in Europe, Africa, Russia, and the Far East, and to catch the feeling of the rest of the world toward America. These experiences can transform his preaching. It would be wonderful if the two of them could take such trips together, but this is not always possible. Sometimes children cannot be left at home without their mother, and often finances cannot be stretched to cover two. But this fact should not keep the minister from traveling. The wife who sets her foot firmly on the proposition, "He's not going till he can take me with him," is not only being selfish; she is betraying a basic lack of understanding of the importance of travel to the ministry her husband must render. These are days when the Christian faith must be interpreted in terms of global movements. It is, of course, possible for a man to keep his finger on the pulse of the world through his reading and his conversations with others; but anyone who has traveled knows that when the element of personal experience is added to what one reads or hears, new light is revealed and conviction is born.

2. Accept your responsibilities as a mother. Not all ministers have children, to be sure, but families are not uncommon in parsonages, and when the children are small they constitute their mother's first responsibility. This is a responsibility not to be shared with her husband when he should be calling or in the study. Not only the minister but also the laymen are embarrassed when he must postpone an afternoon call because he is baby-sitting while his wife is at the women's meeting. It is no better for her to bring the children to the church and deposit them in his study where he can "keep an eye on them while he works." If he keeps an eye on them, he won't do much work. Laymen's wives cannot impose on their husband's employment in this manner, and neither should the minister's wife.

As the children grow, she, more than anyone else, will determine their attitude toward their father and the church. If she complains that he is never home and groans at word of another meeting, the children will catch her mood. If, on the other hand, the children see she loves the church and thinks it is worth sacrificing for, that she is proud of her husband and believes in the nobility of his calling, they will react in like manner.

3. Maintain a positive attitude about your own job. The work of a minister's wife is a profession in its own right. There is no reason why a minister's wife cannot love her job just as much as her husband loves his. Yet a disproportionate number of ministers' wives become bitter. They grow negative in their reactions and are quick to express resentments. They resent living in a parsonage and furnishing their home under the direction of a parsonage committee. They resent the church and its constant demands. They resent their husband's busy schedule. They resent church people, and often put the worst interpretation on well-meant actions. Bristling with bitterness, they prejudice their children against the church and drag their husbands down to defeat.

They accommodate themselves to their own bitterness in different ways. Some of them have a compulsion to work all the harder to cover the guilt they feel for their resentment. With this compulsive hyperactivity they lose their sensitivity to other people and cause a good deal of trouble around the church. Others go to the opposite extreme and declare they will do in the church what they happen to enjoy, and nothing more. Other wives express their resentment by making unreasonable demands of their husbands. Feeling in competition with the church, they take a kind of delight in getting their husbands to serve them. Because the minister's hours are more flexible than the hours of many other people, they can easily impose on their husbands to run errands, baby-sit, fix meals, and do dishes. In the interest of a happy home, some ministers submit to this kind of demand. Still other wives break with their minister's-wife vocation more dramatically by taking a job on their own. Occasionally this is a financial necessity, to pay extensive bills, to put children through college, to finance a trip abroad, or just to supplement a woefully inadequate ministerial salary. But sometimes it is an expression of a rejection of the role of a minister's wife.

All the while that the minister's wife is nursing her bitterness she is missing the diamonds in her own yard. Few vocations offer such a multitude of satisfactions as may be found in the role she is called upon to play. In what other profession can there be such a grand partnership of a woman with her husband and family? What other job will guarantee such a host of ready-made friends to welcome one to a new community? And in what other position can one find such a multitude of well-wishers and friendly helping hands? Many people are bored for lack of anything worth-while to do. The minister's wife is blessed with numerous opportunities every day for rendering constructive service or a word of cheer to someone else. Other people are often uncertain, especially when they come to a new community, to know where to turn for professional services. The minister's wife has access to the services of the best doctors, lawyers, and dentists, often without charge. Many people are circumscribed by their own narrow social group. A minister's wife has the exciting experience of mingling with all types of people. Some women have little opportunity to express their femininity. They have no one to mother, no one to love, no one to entertain. The minister's wife has all the challenge anyone could want to her motherly instinct, and besides her family she has a whole congregation to love and call hers in a special way. Besides this she has a rare opportunity to express her feminine skills of cooking, flower arranging, and entertaining, as she has a formal dinner for visiting dignitaries one day and a party for the junior department the next.

Many people envy the minister's wife. Many girls hope to marry a minister. Let the minister's wife, therefore, rise to the full stature of her position, and learn to love her work as her husband loves his. And let her be to her husband both a sweetheart and a wise companion. Who can do so much as she to lift her husband's discouragement, quiet his anxiety, and give him courage? In his dramatic account of his work in directing the Montgomery bus strike, Martin Luther King pays tribute to such a wife. He writes, "I seldom knew from one hour to the next when I would be home. Many times Coretta saw her good meals grow dry in the oven when a sudden emergency kept me away. Yet she never complained, and she was always there when I needed her. 'Yoki' [their small daughter] and Beethoven, she said, kept her company when she was alone. Calm and unruffled, Coretta moved quietly about the business of keeping the household going. When I needed to talk things out, she was ready to listen, or to offer suggestions when I asked for them. Her fortitude was my strength. Afraid for me at times, she never allowed her fears to worry me or impede my work in the protest."[5]

My wife, too, is my ministry's richest blessing. God's greatest gift to a minister is such a wife.

VII

DISCIPLINED DISORDER

❖ ❖ ❖

In his Yale Lectures, John Henry Jowett said this:

Be as systematic as a business-man. Enter your study at an appointed hour, and let that hour be as early as the earliest of your business-men goes to his warehouse or his office. I remember in my earlier days how I used to hear the factory operatives passing my house on the way to the mills, where work began at six o'clock. I can recall the sound of their iron-clogs ringing through the street. The sound of the clogs fetched me out of bed and took me to my work. I no longer hear the Yorkshire clogs, but I can see and hear my business-men as they start off early to earn their daily bread. And shall their minister be behind them in his quest of the Bread of Life? Shall he slouch and loiter into the day, shamed by those he assumes to lead, and shall his indolence be obtrusive in the services of the sanctuary when "the hungry sheep look up and are not fed?" Let the minister, I say, be as business-like as the business-man. Let him employ system and method, and let him be as scrupulously punctual in his private habits in the service of his Lord, as he would have to be in a government-office in the service of his country.[1]

That's a ringing challenge, and the minister in whom it inspires no resolution is well-nigh past redemption. Only the highly disciplined personality can meet the demands of a worthy pulpit.

But, often as not, the resolution to enter the study earlier and to apply to one's sermon all the techniques of the skilled artisan or devoted artist is followed by disillusionment. Beating the dawn to the study door is well and good if one can make it to bed before the first cock starts its crowing. But one does not have to pull himself from his pillow at an early hour many mornings before he realizes that if this "discipline" is to work he must adjust his habits at the other side of the darkness as well. Possibly, as some say, we can get along with less sleep than we think we require, but somewhere there is a limit, and there is little to be gained by meeting the morning deadline if one is too dull to be creative.

The problem is that not all of the minister's responsibilities can be harnessed to the same discipline. To be sure, the preparation of good sermons requires one to arrive at his study fresh and at an appointed hour; and if one is to do consistently good work, he should keep his study time free from interruptions. But good work as a pastor and an administrator requires something quite different. The man who would counsel with students, for example, needs to be free when students are free, and when they are in a mood to "talk"—which is usually at night, the later the better. And the man who would mastermind an organization that is smooth and efficient soon learns that there is no time like the morning to catch others in their offices, and to solicit co-operative participation. By afternoon people have scattered. They are hard to find in, and they are burdened down with a day that has grown too heavy. In addition, many of the minister's responsibilities defy every attempt to schedule them. Important calls come at unpredictable moments, and often the interruption turns out to be the main business. A man may resent the knock at his study door when he is trying to get his sermon finished before reviewing the agenda for the evening meeting and leaving for an afternoon conference in the Council of Churches office; but if the visitor has come to the minister in the desperate hope of finding someone who will understand and help him, the minister is forced to ask himself if this "intrusion" is not really his door of opportunity. As he spends an hour or two with this seeker after truth, his neatly arranged and tightly packed schedule goes out the window.

This conflict between discipline and disorder in his life constitutes one of the most persistent and defiant problems the minister faces. It keeps him almost perpetually on the horns of a dilemma. Adhering to disciplines that are too strict, he is in danger of sacrificing something of the warmth of personality that we like to associate with the ministry. Giving himself too freely to his people, on call twenty-four hours a day, and "glad to see anyone any time," he is sure to become as shallow as he is agreeable.

Like most of the other problems discussed in this book, this one has its roots in our confused concept of what the ministry is. One has to know what he wants to accomplish before he can develop an effective discipline for accomplishing it. When a man starts to write a sermon, one of the first things he should do is to write out a simple statement of the aim of that sermon. This gives direction and prevents digression. Similarly, when a man starts his ministerial career, he would be well advised to write out a simple statement of the aim of his ministry. Life's fundamental discipline is to know where you are going. After that has been clarified, the question of organization or disorder is more or less a matter of individual differences. There have been successful ministers whose desks were always neat and organized, who answered their mail with dispatch, and who were punctual in meeting every appointment. And there have been successful ministers who were careless at all these points. But there has never been a great minister who had a fuzzy or uncertain concept of what his main business was about.

Perhaps the crux of the matter is in the distinction between discipline and order. "Disciplined disorder" is not necessarily a contradiction in terms. It is possible, indeed very common, for a highly disciplined person to be disorderly, especially in certain areas of his experience. And it is both possible and common for a person who is meticulous about every detail to lack a basic sense of discipline. The person who is disciplined but disorderly may be the one who has such a well-defined goal to which he is devoted with such singleness of heart that he can't be bothered with the details that clutter the lives of less-well-oriented personalities. The person who is orderly but undisciplined may be the one who, being caught up in no absorbing life goal, compensates by being overly devoted to meticulous detail. For some people, too much attention to detail is an escape mechanism. Absorbed in sorting cards and keeping graphs, one can escape the more rigorous discipline of fighting one's way through big theological problems or working out complicated interpersonal relations.

But hold steady. Don't leap to the notion that carelessness about detail is an indication your mind is moving in a higher realm. It may mean only that you are lazy. Remember that the highly disciplined person is not careless about the detail that is directly related to his main goal. He simply has gained the maturity which enables him to be casual about the kinds of details that are *popularly thought* to be important, and conscientious about the details that *are* important.

That leads us into the first of two suggestions I want to make to the person who finds himself struggling with the problems of discipline and disorder: he should recognize that a stern discipline is a requisite to quality. He may attain eminence without it, but not greatness. To be sure, undisciplined ministers are sometimes thrust into positions of prominence and even of power beyond what they deserve or are capable of handling. This is because the choice of leaders is so often in the hands of persons who are themselves undisciplined. But such an elevation in rank is no honor. The true goal of the ministry is high quality, not high rank. In attaining this goal there is no substitute for discipline.

Discipline means an eye that is not distracted from the goal: it means faithfulness to an appointed task; it means discrimination in the use of time; it means rejection of the good when there is a better; it means self-denial and drudgery. Daniel Webster put it plainly in his advice to lawyers. He said, "A man can never gallop over the fields of law on Pegasus, nor fly across them on the wing of oratory. —If he would stand on terra firma, he must descend. —If he would be a great lawyer, he must first consent to become a great drudge."

Any worth-while venture comes at the price of disciplined labor. Thus novelist John P. Marquand describes what it is like to finish a book by saying, "I feel a deep sense of relief— the species of relief that occurs many times daily in the maternity ward of any hospital." And Althea Gibson, accounting for her success in the world of sports, says, "If I made it, it's half because I was game enough to take an awful lot of punishment along the way." Similarly, Irvin Cobb shattered the illusions of those who think that writing is easy to produce because it is easy to read. "You ought to see me some morning," he wrote, "when I'm dashing off my stuff—about one inch an hour."

In the hard work, long hours, persistent practice, and disappointing setbacks that form the prelude to achievement, the ministry is no different from any other field. Harry Emerson Fosdick describes his experience in learning to preach as "a struggle," and adds, "Preaching for me has never been easy, and at the start it was often exceedingly painful."

There is nothing more satisfying in human experience than creative achievement such as the production of fine music, the writing of a worth-while book, or the preaching of a great sermon. But anyone who has reached the goal in any of these fields knows that, but for the grace of God and his own dogged determination to stay by a rigorously imposed self-discipline, his dream would have miscarried. Most of us resist hard work. Mental exertion in particular is avoided at the slightest excuse. Not only the reluctant high-school student who doesn't see what good his French is going to do him anyway, but also the Christian minister at his study desk, is tempted to piddle with every diversion that will postpone the mind's struggle with ideas. Joshua Reynolds once wrote: "There is no expedient to which a man will not resort to avoid the real labor of thinking." Describing the persistence with which she must fight off tempting alternatives to writing, Helga Sandburg tells of the small bird that appears at her study window, capturing her attention: "He is a curious one. In a moment, though, he goes away and I have to write. I would rather wash windows or start a ragout, weed the flowers or bake bread." No doubt Miss Sandburg would agree with J. Edgar Park's assertion that "one of the most impassable roads in the world is that between the brain and the point of a pen." Anyone who thinks that a writer picks up his pen just because he loves it does not know the whole story. A love for it is present, of course. But so also is a determined grip on the pen that, like Jacob's wrestle with the angel, will not let go until a blessing has been released.

But most people find that something more than love of the task and a determination to see it through is necessary. This additional element is orderliness. Presently, as we have already hinted, we will look at the other side of the coin, but for the moment let's examine the virtues of a professional life that fits into well-defined categories and knows the firm ribs of structure. One writer says it for all of us when she confesses, "I find a schedule imperative. There is the tendency in me to dawdle and a routine snaps me up."

Phillips Brooks said it for the ministers: "Do not be tempted by the fascination of spontaneousness. Do not be misled by any delusion of inspiration. No one dreads mechanical woodenness in the ministry more than I do. And yet a set of well-framed and well-joined habits about times and ways of work, writing, studying, association with people, the administration of charity and education, and the proportions between the different departments of clerical labor, is

again and again the bridge over which the minister walks
where the solid ground of higher motive fails him for a time.
Routine is a terrible master, but she is a servant whom we can
hardly do without."[2]

There is scarcely a phase of the ministerial calling that cannot be improved through the application of system. Even the
creative process of sermon preparation has its mechanical
side. Thought proceeds best through known and widely accepted stages. Many people from different walks of life have
outlined the steps that lead to the production of something
worth-while—a poem, a novel, a sermon, an invention, a
mathematical conclusion or scientific discovery. They express
it in different words, but they all come out about the same
place. All include such stages as (1) gathering the raw material, picking up ideas and illustrations; (2) living with the
stuff gathered, organizing and reorganizing it, rejecting it, and
embracing it again; (3) a period of incubation when the work
is turned over to the subconscious while one goes about other
business; (4) the inspiration—the illumination—the birth of
the creative idea; (5) the period of verification and shaping of
the idea for practical use.

While these stages are not always clear-cut, and often take
place simultaneously, they nevertheless indicate that even
"just thinking," if it is to be productive, must follow a pattern.
And it must be nailed into place or it will escape. The truth
of this is indicated in a bit of dialogue from Lewis Carroll's
Through The Looking Glass:

"The horror of that moment," the King went on, "I shall
never, NEVER forget!"

"You will, though," the Queen said, "if you don't make a
memorandum of it."

Rudolf Flesch states it firmly: "Once the idea is born,
tips are unnecessary—except one: WRITE IT DOWN. The best
idea is useless if it is lost and forgotten. Catch your ideas alive.
Keep a notebook handy; if you don't have a notebook, find a

pad; if you can't find a pad, use an old envelope. But don't let the idea get away. It may never come back."

System is necessary in sermon preparation, and the orderliness should find its way into the sermon itself. This is not a text book on homiletics, but it is in order to say that the minister who never learns to structure his sermons seldom preaches with clarity and persuasiveness. For a time I taught homiletics in a theological seminary. The summer before I began my teaching I was in Chicago, and made it a point to see Dean Charles Gilkey, to ask what counsel he would give to a young man starting to teach this important and often neglected subject. He said, "Have the boys outline, outline, outline!" No one should be timid about revealing the points of his sermon to the congregation. People appreciate having pegs on which to hang their ideas. A well-outlined speech is easier to understand, and is remembered longer.

But it is important to be systematic in more things than sermon preparation. Even a minister's letters and telephone conversations can stand some outlining in order to be made more effective. For instance, a minister may call someone whom he wants to secure as the speaker for an annual church banquet, and say something like this: "Dr. Evans? This is Peter Smith at the First Baptist Church. I am calling to see if you will speak at our annual banquet, January fifteenth?" Then he may proceed to describe the nature of the banquet, the subject matter requested, and the length of speech desired. All of that information is easy to assimilate because the minister who called first specified what it was he was after. But suppose he had begun the conversation in this manner: "Dr. Evans? Will you be busy January fifteenth?" Immediately the good Doctor is put on the spot. He has no idea what is to follow, and doesn't know whether to plan to be busy that night or not. The minister's relationship with Dr. Evans is off to a bad start. It pays off to think through a telephone conversation in advance, and approach it in a logical manner.

Or take a business letter. Some people may like to get a long and involved letter in order to spend as much time as possible with their mail. As for myself, I much prefer to receive a letter that starts out, "Dear Mr. Walker: We are pleased you have accepted our invitation to be with us the week of February 3rd. (That's the introduction.) There are three things relative to this engagement that we want to call to your attention. (That's what is known in homilitical parlance as the "propositional sentence.") Then there might follow in three brief, neat paragraphs a discussion of the matters involved. It is exceedingly important, in getting ideas over to people, to have them clearly outlined and specifically stated.

Nowhere does the habit of carefully outlined ideas pay off more than in administrative work. Most people are willing to accept a responsibility assigned to them, if they can see clearly what it is. The longer I live, the more convinced I am that much of the time our organizational activities fall down, not because people are unwilling to accept responsibility, nor because they are not interested, but because no one has given them a clear-cut outline, which cannot possibly be misunderstood, of what is expected of them.

Now we must confront a practical problem. If the minister is going to work with the kind of precision we have been talking about, he must create a setting which makes it possible. It takes large blocks of uninterrupted time to outline and write a good sermon. And it is quite impossible for a man to come to a meeting with every detail thought through and prepared for in advance if he has been too busy with other, possibly important, but unrelated matters. He needs a time and a place to do his "homework."

The church office seldom meets the need. It is a good place to meet people and attend to business matters, but it leaves something to be desired as a retreat for creative planning or sermon preparation. Actually, the minister faces two distinct and very different needs, and the same room will not do for both. He needs both a study and an office, not an office that doubles as a study. The requirements of the two are almost diametrically opposed. The office should be near other church offices and as accessible to the public as possible; the study should be in a remote spot, not available to visitors. The office should have a busy telephone; the study should have no telephone at all. The office should contain administrative files, guidebooks, parish maps, denominational journals, dictating equipment, and the like. The study should be free of all these distractions, and contain instead the minister's library and his sermon-preparation files.

To some people this will sound like an impossible dream. They can't even find one adequate room to double as office and study, and the possibility of locating two is so remote as to be laughable. But the idea ought not to be dismissed too lightly. A man's work can be greatly improved with this kind of an arrangement, and most laymen are interested in helping their minister do a better job. There are few communities, even small ones, that do not have somewhere an unused room that can be fitted out as a study for the preacher, and such rooms can often be made available at little or no cost.

Under the pressure of the need, many men have worked out arrangements that have proved to be satisfactory to them. Some have an office at the church and their study at home. Others find that even when a room at home is available it does not serve the purpose. It is too difficult to keep the children away from the study door, and too hard on the minister's wife to hold off persons who want to get through to the minister, knowing that he is in the house. And even when the children dutifully stay away, and the wife proves to be a real guard, the minister may hear so much of the noise of ringing phones and conversations explaining he isn't available that he might just as well accept the interruptions and be done with it.

Some men find a room in some remote spot in the church—

in the tower or basement—that fits the bill. Here they set up their study, not worrying about fancy furniture or modern decoration. Most churches have at least one or two elderly couples or widows living quietly in large homes that are now only half used. If they knew the minister needed a room for his private study, they would more than likely be flattered to be asked to make a room in their home available to him. Harry Emerson Fosdick maintained a study in an office building. No one but his wife knew where he was to be found, and she interrupted him only in extreme emergencies. As for myself, I have tried most of the methods mentioned, but finally have taken the leaf from Dr. Fosdick's notebook and, through the kindness of the local Y.M.C.A., have set up my study in a room in a quiet and little-used section of the building. This is the most satisfactory arrangement I have ever had. Few people know where I am located, and those who do respect my need for privacy.

I have often thought that ministers might be of help to one another in this regard. The Huntington Hartford Foundation has provided a retreat for writers, painters, composers, and other artists in a beautiful canyon not far from Sunset Boulevard in Los Angeles. Sixteen cabins scattered about on the slopes are made available to qualified persons who need to get away to a quiet spot to do creative work. There they enjoy fulfillment of the dream of everyone who creates: uninterrupted privacy. The one rule that must be obeyed by all is that no one interrupts anyone else during working hours unless he has been previously invited to do so. I know of no such facilities available to ministers, but I should think that if the minister of a large church with a number of unused rooms extended an invitation to ministers within a reasonable radius to set up a study in his building, with the guarantee they would have complete privacy, he would find a happy response.

So much, then, for the challenge to live an orderly life if one is going to achieve quality in his ministry. Now I want to swing to the other element in this problem and remind the reader that in spite of the need for systematic planning and organization, disorder is sometimes in order. We have already mentioned the fact that it is possible for a disciplined person to be disorderly. Now let's explore that idea a little.

Recently the University of California Institute of Personality Assessment and Research made a study of types of people who function best under trying conditions. Included in a radio report of their findings were these provocative words: "Something else is required before we can say that a person has achieved the highest level of integration or psychological health. And that is the ability to permit oneself to become disorganized." Orderliness is commendable, but if one is so tied to routine and so bound by system that he is frustrated when he gets outside of it, his passion for organization has become a compulsion and is a disease rather than a virtue.

While it is true that some people never preach well because they never learn to outline, it is also true that some are such slaves to exact classification and neat development of points that the rushing wind of the spirit is squeezed right out of their sermons. Rudolf Flesch warns that "there is such a thing as a too strict classification or a too orderly outline," and counsels, "If you are the kind of person who loves neat card files, try dropping all your cards on the floor sometime. It will do you no end of good. Or if you are used to starting every writing job by making an outline, don't. Wait until you have felt the click. Before that, any outline will tie your ideas down." And it is interesting to note that Helga Sandburg, the same writer who said, "I find a schedule imperative" and "a routine snaps me up," refers to her desk as "the confusion before me," and comments, "Purposely I am not tidy."

The minister who browses in books that are not on his reading list, wastes on a TV show an evening he had planned to devote to study, or spontaneously accepts a friendly invitation to go bowling on an afternoon that might have been given to calling is likely to discover a dimension of life that is hidden from the man who is too unbending in his routine. And it may turn out that the chance comment or interesting incident that comes to light at one of these not-in-the-schedule times when his mind is in neutral will turn out to be the making of a sermon. Even the minister who sticks strictly to a timetable is likely to note, if he is flexible enough to be observing, that many of his best illustrations come from those in-between moments when he is employed with nothing more constructive than getting from one place to another. "Flying from New York to Denver, last week, our plane ran into trouble" is a come-on that is likely to arouse a good deal more interest in the average audience than is a sentence that begins, "In his book on Christian doctrine, one noted theologian says . . ."

Routine makes for dependability, but a nonscheduled flight with fun adds freshness. Bookkeeping fits well into office hours, but creative art is likely to play hooky from school. Although, with a reasonable amount of gray matter, one can grasp the intricacies of theology in time to pass an examination, the Holy Spirit seldom arrives on schedule, and insight is as likely to strike in the swimming pool as in the study. In *The Art of Clear Thinking*, Rudolf Flesch gives some of the answers a group of research chemists came up with when they were asked when and how their scientific insights came:

"While dodging automobiles across Park Row and Broadway, New York."
"Sunday in church as the preacher was announcing the text."
"At three o'clock in the morning."
"In the evening when alone in the study room."
"In the morning when shaving."
"In the early morning while in bed."
"Just before and just after an attack of gout."
"Late at night after working intensively for some hours."
"Invariably at night after retiring for sleep."

"In the plant one Sunday morning about 9 A.M. when no one was around."

"While riding in a very early train to another city."

"While resting and loafing on the beach."

"While sitting at my desk doing nothing, and thinking about other matters."

"After a month's vacation, as I was dressing after a bath in the sea."[3]

If it proves nothing else, this list at least indicates that great ideas have slight respect for a man's schedule. J. Robert Oppenheimer says flatly that "Theoretical insights flourish best when the thinker is apparently wasting time." It is for this reason that the organizational frame of mind fits so awkwardly across the ways of the creative thinker. William H. Whyte, Jr., is talking about the administrator (and there is no reason to exclude the church administrator) when he says, "The creative individual he does not understand, nor does he understand the conditions of creativity. The messiness of intuition, the aimless thoughts, the unpractical questions—all these things that are so often the companion to discovery are anathema to the world of the administrator. Order, objective goals, agreement—these are his desiderata."

And this brings us to a direct encounter with the human problem of this chapter. The minister, seeking to be both the administrator and the creative artist, is likely to be perpetually at war with himself. Swinging into the station on schedule, he may chafe at the routine and long to be free from the rails he rides. But he is not likely to be free from restrictions for long before he looks with longing toward a more ordered existence and feels an urge to whip things into line. This is as it should be. What he must look for is proportion. Wisdom is not found either in order or disorder, but in a proper balance between the two. The minister must have that combination of managerial skills and creative insights that goes to make up a true leader. In an article on "Leadership," reprinted from the

Royal Bank of Canada Monthly Letter, this interesting sentence appears: "Many a sad story is written in the annals of business every year by leaders who are falling into the routine of being managers." That happens to preachers too.

I suspect it is most likely to happen to those who habitually give the best part of the day, when their minds are freshest, to handling organizational routine, and do their creative work when they are sluggish. No matter how carefully or how carelessly the rest of his hours are scheduled, a wise minister will find out when he is at his best mentally, and will set that time aside for study in preparation for his preaching. The best time varies with different people. Ernest Hemingway works best in the early morning hours. John O'Hara found he was most creative after midnight. Katherine Brush discovered two creative periods, one in the morning and another in the evening. And Arnold Toynbee reports, "I write every morning, whether I am in the mood or not. I sit down to write straightaway after breakfast, before dealing with my correspondence or any other business, and I do this writing at home. Then I go for lunch to the Royal Institute of International Affairs, and, in my office there, from after lunch till 6:45, dictate my letters, see people, do my work in editing the Institute's political history of the war, and do my writing for this history as well. In fact, I give half my day to one job and half to another, and find refreshment in switching my mind to and fro in this way."[4]

Probably Toynbee's schedule corresponds rather closely with that of most preachers. But let every man work this out for himself, remembering that if he wants to preach with effectiveness, his best hours should be given to preparation for it.

In the last analysis, then, the way a man orders his life is an individual matter and may not be of too much importance. But the way he disciplines his life is of profound importance. He can accomplish great things on schedule or off, but without a disciplined purpose and drive, his little rocket isn't likely to get off the ground. Bishop Kennedy, speaking about men who are always going to write a book but never do, says, "This kind of achievement is possible only for the man who gets up in the morning before other men arise and goes to bed at night after most men have retired. Above all, it is done only by the man who seats himself and begins to write." And the author of the article on "Leadership" puts it on the line for all of us when he says, "Leaders are so eager about their work that they can hardly wait for morning to get started at it. But they are not impetuous. They keep a balance between emotional drive and sound thinking. Their excess of effort testifies to their belief that unless a man undertakes more than he possibly can do he will never do all that he can do. Their enthusiasm stimulates their energy."

VIII

DENOMINATIONALLY ECUMENICAL

❖ ❖ ❖

One Sunday morning the First Christian Church in Corvallis, Oregon, was invaded by Methodist doctrine. No one quite knows how it happened; but when the members who were accustomed to using hearing aids turned on their instruments, they did not hear their own pastor, who was standing before them in the pulpit. Instead, they heard the minister of The First Methodist Church six blocks away. The Methodist service was broadcast by radio, and somehow the Christian Church hearing aids picked up the signal.

Admittedly this is a rather bizarre method of achieving ecumenicity, but it is about as effective as most inter-denominational ventures the average minister has a chance to participate in.

Great things are being done through the National and World Councils of Churches, but the movement is weak and unconvincing where it touches the local pastor. The denominations meet together to confess the error of a divided church, and return to strengthen the divisions they decry. They organize a local Council of Churches as an expression of their unity in Christ and give it no more than the token support they would extend to any worth-while but more or less irrelevant venture.

Denominationalism doesn't mean much to most laymen any more. A man can be a good Presbyterian in Los Angeles and a happy Methodist when he moves to Detroit. It depends pretty much on who is in the pulpit, what kind of a program is available for his children, and how convenient the parking is. Every minister knows that when he goes out to call on his "prospects" he can expect to visit in the homes of people from a variety of denominations, including the Roman Catholic. "We are broad-minded," they say, with an air that suggests they feel a little sorry for the minister who isn't as free as they to transfer from denomination to denomination to experience first hand the contribution each has to offer. And, indeed, there is good reason to reflect on this. It may be that the transferring layman is getting a wider, richer experience of churchmanship than is available to the minister who, with retirement benefits and professional advancement at stake, is bound for life to one denomination.

Meanwhile, self-conscious denominational leaders dig into their history to see what "archaeological" treasures they can unearth. They reprint ancient volumes that set forth their church's peculiar doctrines or theological twists, and they resurrect the great personages of their denomination's early days and stimulate a revival of interest in their biographies, busts, and blunders. Old orders of worship, long since abandoned or modified by those who found them inadequate, are brought back into current use with the fiction that they are somehow more theologically sound than something a modern churchman could devise. Talking boldly of church union, but preoccupied with their own denominational history, they are behaving very much like a frustrated young woman who, desiring marriage, is afraid of it, and meets the challenge by making a study of her family tree.

It is a strange and even ridiculous state of affairs, and the minister is caught in the center of it. The simultaneous thrust toward church union and revival of denominationalism often focuses on the pastor's desk. He is counseled to teach his people about the World Church, but to use his denominational literature to do it. He must guide them in understanding that we are all a part of the one true Church of Christ, and then whip up their enthusiasm to be loyal Lutherans or Congregationalists or Episcopalians. He quite naturally has a bias in favor of his own denomination, which, in all probability, has nurtured him in his early religious growth, provided him with a theological education, and given him a church to serve. He is fond of his church leaders and wants to co-operate with them in every way. But the ecumenical bug has bitten him and he wants to do something more constructive about it than merely to read the accounts of high-level conversations on the subject.

Not many opportunities are open to him, however. There have been a few genuine "united Protestant churches" developed in the country, but most of these, like the church at Richland, Washington, and Park Forest, Illinois, have been in new communities and under circumstances which applied uncommonly strong pressures on the denominations to forget their vested interests and co-operate in a common endeavor. Members of these churches are enthusiastic about the projects and show a great deal more pride in the fact that sectarianism is not an issue with them than they ever previously had in the denominations they came from. They clearly think of themselves as belonging to the church of the future.

In the well-established communities, however, united Protestant churches are still a long way off, and the minister who wants to work for one is bucking some impressive opposition. Take downtown Oakland, California, for example. It is no doubt typical of dozens of situations across the land. Within a radius of seven blocks, there are six Protestant churches. All but one claim to be the "First Church" of their denomination. That one is the Episcopal Church which doesn't normally use the First Church nomenclature. These churches have a great deal in common. They all have a distinguished history. Most have boasted larger memberships in the past than they claim at present. Most have larger sanctuaries than they have been filling in recent years. They all presume to minister to the entire city and its suburbs. They all have relatively large budgets and a staff of professional workers. All are faced with the problem of whether they should stay on indefinitely in their present location. And all are desirous of being a "Voice Church" in a great metropolitan area.

The problems that confront them are obvious. It is hard for people to find parking nearby, but to buy downtown property to convert into parking lots is a very expensive proposition even if suitably located lots were available. New and modernized facilities are desirable to meet the needs of members and constituents, but the cost of building in a downtown area is much greater than elsewhere. A young and growing church membership in a new residential area can gamble on its future, but a much larger downtown church, where the membership does not increase rapidly and some years even loses ground, is less sure of its future. A metropolitan downtown church should be at least the voice of its denomination, if not of Protestantism, for the area; but to fulfill this role adequately a church must be able to afford radio and television time, and the importance of its witness must be recognized by the civic leaders.

As things stand now, no one of these churches is likely to solve its problems and fully achieve its goals. Of course, there is always the possibility that one or more of them will hit upon the formula that will bring a strong surge in growth and influence. One of the denominations might see the importance of doing something about the situation and pour extensive funds into the enterprise. A wealthy member might leave the church a generous bequest enabling it to advance its program beyond what could be supported by the regular giving of the members. Or the frequently mentioned return to the city may materialize, reversing the population trend and stimulating a boom in the downtown church comparable to the rapid growth the suburban churches have had in recent years. Barring any of these developments, however, these churches, still relatively strong, are likely to go on competing with one another in a dignified sort of way, gaining a little ground one year and losing it the next, rallying their loyal members to a dream of the great future they have in the city, and finally moving out to a residential neighborhood, or dwindling to the fate of a sad old city church that no minister wants to serve.

Of course there is an alternative. They can follow the lead of Richland and Park Forest, and face their future together. Here is a made-to-order opportunity for six churches to combine their forces in the creation of a great Metropolitan Protestant Temple. In a united effort, pooling the resources they have tied up in six separate expensive city properties, they could build a structure that would not be dwarfed by the towering new Kaiser Building in the neighborhood. They could undoubtedly have access to additional funds that would be made available to a united effort, but withheld from denominational drives. Such a united church could command the staff each separate church has dreamed about having, and yet release a few of the ministers (there are twenty of them) now tied up in these separate enterprises to serve other places where ministers are so badly needed. It could be in truth the Protestant Christian Center for the area, and the voice of Protestantism in the city and beyond. It could wield an influence in city, county, and state government that could not be touched by any single denomination, and it could advance ecumenicity by a long stride.

But of course this isn't about to happen. No one is even seriously proposing it. Why? Because the denominations won't let it happen. They resisted it in Park Forest until the pressures were too overwhelming to cope with. The mere fact that a majority of the people preferred a united church wasn't convincing in itself. When the movement first got under way,

"The denominations didn't think much of the idea," William H. Whyte, Jr., reports, and adds, "A fight there had to be, but before long, worn down by the sheer pressure of mass meetings, petitions of one kind or another (and some scoldings from the *Christian Century*), the denominations agreed to compromise."

And unfortunately, a compromise is exactly what most denominations consider a united effort to be. Each is sure it has nothing to gain and everything to lose by any sort of "union," "federation," or "community" of local churches. Local churches can join together in some creative venture only through the support of the denominations of which they are a part. These denominations are actively engaged in conversations about ecumenicity on the world level, but they are frightened speechless at the suggestion that a local church would like to work out its own future in union with the churches of other denominations in the same area. Good will among the churches they will readily applaud, and they will not object to co-operation on a limited number of interdenominational programs. But the idea that a church might find its life by losing it they find distinctly heretical.

Sometimes I think that the old war between the denominations, when each knew what it stood for and challengingly erected an edifice across the street from its competitor with the deliberate intent of proselytizing, bespoke greater religious vitality than is evidenced in our current acceptance of one another as "separate but equal."

At any rate, most ministers won't find direct efforts toward unions of local churches very profitable business. They will need to look elsewhere for opportunities to express their growing urge toward unity. The obvious place to turn is to the Council of Churches and other voluntary interdenominational relationships. Unfortunately, however, few ministers will find anything to challenge them in the usual round of co-operative church endeavors. Radio programs sponsored by

Councils of Churches and ministerial associations are next to useless. This is because the accepted pattern is to take turns the way children do in kindergarten. It is as though the great mission of the church were to show the public we can play together rather than to challenge a pagan society with a redeeming gospel. I suppose there are people who faithfully listen to the ministerial association's evening meditations as a radical Methodist follows a ritualistic Episcopalian who was preceded by a free-wheeling Nazarene, but I never met one. The best most people do is to learn when their pastor is to be heard on the program and tune in to get more of the same thing they get on Sunday morning. This kind of inter-denominational programming doesn't declare our unity; it emphasizes our divisions. If the churches want to do something together on the radio or on television, let them find the person, minister or layman, who can best communicate the gospel to secular society, and let him be the featured personality on the program each time. Some notable programs of this type have been tried with conspicuous success, and come much closer to what we should be doing together than taking turns.

Radio is not the only area in which our attempts to work together have been too self-conscious. Good Friday services are just as bad. Fortunately most people don't stay through for the full three hours. This saves them from the shattering experience of seeing a sacred vigil turned into a theological grab bag. In the average Good Friday service which employs the services of seven different preachers (some of whom have been racing breathlessly from the First Word at the Third Presbyterian Church to the Third Word at the First Baptist), there is such divergence of method, interpretation, and ability as to make one wonder if some got in by mistake.

Occasionally a Council of Churches or other duly constituted interdenominational body sponsors a great mass meeting, bringing in some noted figure as the featured speaker of the occasion. Enthusiasm for the chosen headliner is seldom uniform. Sometimes there is organized opposition to him and the unity is again threatened. And more often than not, when the mass meeting is held, the local preachers share the platform with the visitor and exhibit their denominational wares by giving the invocation, reading the scripture, receiving the offering, and pronouncing the benediction. This is another demonstration of the unity that insists on making us stand out as representatives of separate denominations.

No one has a harder job than a Council of Churches executive. Everyone believes in the ideal he represents, but few have time to spend on it. If a minister does all his own denomination expects of him, he has little time for the Council. And laymen who are carrying a full load in their own church tend to give only fragments of their time and energy to matters concerning interchurch co-operation. Perhaps this is more true of Methodists than of others. Bishop Gerald Ensley has pointed out that "the sense of need for ecumenical fellowship is weak in us as a collective group. . . . The average Methodist simply feels no imperative to ecumenical participation, at least not with the urgency that impels him to attend his annual conference or support World Service." In explaining some of the reasons for this, he says, "For one thing, the desire to ecumenicity which other communions feel is largely met for the Methodists within our own denominational family. We are a world church. We encompass within our fellowship wide and fruitful diversities of faith and practice. After a person has attended his quarterly conference, his annual conference, his jurisdictional conference, the General Conference, and the World Methodist Conference—as some of us did in 1956—his cup of ecumenicity is nearly full." He also points out that it is more difficult for a denomination with a highly centralized system of organization to become an integral part of an ecumenical structure than for a more loosely organized church to do so. He sees the Methodist Church as becoming effectively ecumenical only as the movement emerges from "the administrative head of the church, the Council of Bishops." In this connection, he comments, "One of the axioms for getting things done in the Methodist Church is: observe the chain of command—the bishop, the district superintendents, the preacher, the local church. Every Methodist pastor has so much he must do that every proposal which comes other than from above, or comes under the guise of an elective, he lets alone."[1]

I doubt if Methodists are the only ones who find it hard to whip up enthusiasm for the ecumenical projects currently available. Few churches support interchurch ventures with the same dedication they give to the work of their own denomination. Financial involvement tends to be minimal, and as often as not the denomination's representatives on Councils of Churches are people who need to have some job, but can't get along with others within the framework of the local church. It is interesting, and somewhat disheartening, how often a church's representative on the Council is in no position to represent the church at all. Not infrequently an individual who is little known or generally disliked among his fellow church members becomes a big wheel in the Council's machine.

People of this type are easy prey to those denominational leaders who, unlike the reluctant participators we have been describing, are enthusiastic for the movement because they see ecumenicity as an opportunity to capture all Christendom in their theological net. As J. B. Phillips puts it in his preface to *The Young Church In Action*, "There are many with us who insist that the Holy Spirit can only be given through the orthodox channels, by which they usually mean the channels of their own particular Church." He concedes that God is doubtless a God of order, but points out that "at Caesarea, while Peter was still preaching, the Holy Spirit was given unmistakably to pagans who had not yet been baptized, let alone confirmed!" Similarly, Bishop Ensley points out "the exclusiveness of major bodies" within the World Council of Churches, and observes, "At the same time that the World Council as a whole proclaims the unity of Christendom, several of its member denominations repudiate the claims of others to be Christian churches. They read our Lord's petition on the last night of his life that all might be one; and yet they also refuse—in his name—to admit others of his disciples to his table."

Well, all this is ecumenicity, and it is a frustration to the local minister. What is he to do? Shall he let the battle be fought on the national and world levels and give his time to his own local church, or shall he become deeply involved in ecumenicity on the local level? Shall he look forward to some form of church union, or shall he content himself with denominationalism and pass the buck of church union to the next generation? The students on our campuses are interested in it.

Of course every man must answer these questions for himself, and the answers will be different, depending upon where he is and what needs to be done. However, let me suggest a few guideposts that may prove helpful:

1. Remember that no interdenominational effort is worth much if it is made up of weak units. The best guarantee of a strong ecumenical movement is the prior existence of strong denominations and strong local churches. We should not get together because we are too weak to stand alone—$0 + 0 = 0$—but because that which was meant to be a unity can never be content as a diversity. The finest thing most ministers can do for the ecumenical movement is to administer a great program in their own church.

2. Remember that ecumenicity may be expressed in many ways. On the local level we usually associate the movement with the Council of Churches. But it finds expression also in ministerial associations, Y.M.C.A.-sponsored "interchurch"

activities, and every co-operative endeavor between two or more churches. It is also expressed in the attitude of church leaders and the planning of church boards. The First Methodist Church of San Leandro, California, maintains a large bulletin board that carries the caption "There Are Many Fine Churches in San Leandro." This is kept up to date with bulletins and interesting news items from neighboring churches. This, too, is ecumenicity.

3. Remember that each minister who cares about the Christian faith and its message for this generation has an obligation to help shape the church of tomorrow. Some kind of closer unity is in the making. Whether it will be "federal union," such as E. Stanley Jones remommends, complete merger, or some much looser association, no one is as yet prepared to say. It is important, however, that the future be worked out at the grass roots as well as in world and national conferences. For that reason, the local minister should become a part of the Council of Churches in his city and help to form policy and plan a program to make it the effective instrument it can become, and in some localities has become.

4. Remember that the best way to be ecumenical is to be "denominationally ecumenical." The ecumenical movement is not a refuge for persons who are tired of their denominations and want to give them up in favor of some fictional denominational-less church. The Community Church movement projected something of this kind, and its popularity should make clear to us that there are many people who like the idea of being free from a denominational tag. But the circumstances of the religious world are such that as more and more Community Churches began to spring up, and as there began to develop the need for a larger unit to function through, they found themselves taking on more and more of the characteristics of a separate and distinct denomination.

Ecumenicity is a movement of the churches toward The Church. Sometimes the progress seems slow, and individual ministers are tempted to spurn the sluggish machinery of their own denomination and become ecumenical by themselves. But you can't do it that way. First a man must make his peace with his own denomination. Only then is he in a position to lead his church to join with others in the fulfillment of the Master's prayer that they all might be one.

IX

AFRAID TO BE RADICAL

❖ ❖ ❖

Annually every Methodist preacher can expect a call from at least one teacher in the children's division of the church school. Her class is studying the work of the minister, she will explain, and the curriculum calls for a visit from the pastor himself. Whether they consider themselves skilled in children's work or not, most pastors respond to the invitation and spend at least a few minutes with the youngsters. On such occasions I often begin by asking the children what they think the minister does. The answers are illuminating. "He helps people" is usually the first answer and probably the best summary of the composite view of the members of the class. When encouraged to tell how he helps people, they give such answers as, "He calls on people who are sick," "He tells people about God and Jesus," and "He baptizes [they often require help with the word] little babies."

I can't deny what they say, and yet I often come away from those sessions convinced that a child's mental image of a minister is of a man singularly lacking in virility. They sense that "our pastor" is someone quite special, and they covet his friendly smile, but they think of him as being about as harmless as Santa Claus and as controversial as the mailman.

They don't just imagine this. They learn it. It's among the many ideas they pick up from their parents and grandparents and aunts and neighbors and teachers. It doesn't occur to them to ask whether or not all these people know what a minister is.

And it wouldn't do them any good if they did because while the adults don't know, they don't know that they don't know.

So the ministerial stereotype is passed on. And generation after generation of Christians reach adulthood thoroughly brainwashed. They are conditioned to expect their minister to be conservative. That's why it is such a traumatic experience for some laymen when their pastor makes a radical statement or takes sides on a controversial issue. More than a mere difference of opinion is involved. A lifelong pattern of thought is being challenged. If ministers are to be allowed to hold extreme positions and make shocking statements, a man just can't believe in the church any more—or so some people feel. A good many church laymen, taught from the cradle that a minister is a kindly person who helps people, depend on their pastor to buttress their own conservatism. When he fails to do this, they are disillusioned.

All of this has its effect on the minister himself. He doesn't want to shock people. Few men who have chosen the ministry for a vocation find any particular satisfaction in upsetting others just to see them uncomfortable. Yet the prophetic nature of the minister's calling is such that, if he is a true man of God, he *will* shock people whether he wants to or not. Sooner or later he will become the object of opposition if not open condemnation. The kindergartners, studying about their minister, aren't told about this.

Neither do they have the slightest inkling that he is repeatedly faced with a wretched temptation: the urge to muffle his message to save himself strain. It is very hard not to be what people think you are. One breaks the shell of what others expect of him at his own risk. Not everyone who says he wants his minister to be a courageous man of God will put up with him if he becomes one.

We ministers are keenly aware of this. We know what was done to Jesus, and we know that "Christian" is an adjective often used to modify the word "martyr." But we would rather use the stories of the saints who were burned at the stake or fed to the lions as dramatic material to enliven our sermons and build our congregations than use their methods and lose our following. We know that the religion of Jesus, applied to modern society, is revolutionary. But with professional success at stake, most of us are afraid to be radical.

In the face of this fear we are likely to develop one or the other of three personal characteristics: excessive amiability, a contentious spirit, or responsible leadership.

With most of us the urge to be amiable is overwhelming. And many men have accepted it as the principal determinant of their ministry. They are in favor of that which makes for agreeable relations and opposed to that which disturbs. This is their gospel and their life. Never wanting to be caught on either side of a controversial issue, they avoid the great subjects altogether. The only time they ever deal with a real issue is after it has been settled. They are likely to announce such sermon subjects as "The Beauty of the Christian Life," "How to Handle Our Fears," or "Christ's Prescription for Health."

Bishop Kennedy accurately describes a man of this type as one who "never stands with a minority. He never says no when others say yes. . . . He would never think of standing before a community to say, 'I accuse,' or 'I protest!'" And C. Wright Mills paints a picture of the minister few of us want to be, but all of us are tempted to be, when he writes, "Rather than denounce evil, rather than confront agony, the minister goes his amiable way, bringing glad tidings into each and every home."

People like this are so intent upon maintaining perpetual good will that their only standard is equanimity. The only thing they are really prepared to sacrifice for is the prevention of unpleasantness. What they do not realize is that they belong in the category of those who, seeking to save their lives, lose them. Free from struggle, they become flabby. Careful not to offend anyone, they challenge no one. Afraid of making enemies, they lose their friends. Avoiding such controversial subjects as communism, they prove the Communist contention that, at least with some people, religion is an opiate. Seeking to secure their position by pleasing the people, they have misjudged what the people want.

Most laymen don't want a yes-man who agrees with everything they say and sanctions everything they do. Harry Emerson Fosdick has preached consistently to audiences as large as you are likely to find anywhere in the country. People have traveled long distances just to sit in his congregation. But he didn't attract people by promising to please them. He often took the minority position and preached what a majority of his listeners weren't eager to hear. Even during the war he remained an outspoken pacifist, and more than once challenged his government's policy of mass bombings. Once he vigorously protested a five-to-four decision of the Supreme Court, and praised the minority opinion as it was expressed by Justice Charles E. Hughes. One of the leading lawyers in the church "stalked out and never came back." But Dr. Fosdick says simply, "I should be ashamed to have preached to such congregations without awakening hostility."

Contrast that attitude with the spirit of ministers and laymen on the board of a Methodist hospital in the Midwest. During the war they refused to accept Nisei girls in their nursing school. When asked for an explanation of this policy, they said they were waiting to see how the community was going to react. No true minister of Jesus Christ cuts his convictions to fit community feeling nor does he trim his message to the shape of his congregation. And no congregation worth addressing wants him to.

Writing of the "Plight of Professors During the 'Difficult Years'" when every teacher's loyalty was suspect, Louis M. Hacker said, "Within the classrooms (in part because they were distrustful of their students!) teachers qualified, equivocated, and compromised their work and personal integrity;

outside, they withdrew from the community at large, eschewing political participation and public appearances and giving up subscriptions to magazines and memberships in organizations that were looked upon as in a way non-conformist." We regret the circumstances that stimulated this response, but we regret also the response. Whether in the teaching profession or the ministry, few people admire the person who, holding convictions, is afraid to stand by them in the face of opposition.

Probably more than they realize, and more than the rest of us have stopped to assess, excessively amiable preachers are a threat to the very existence of the church. These are revolutionary times and the world is looking for *leadership*. If the ministers of Jesus Christ don't offer it, someone else will and the church will be dismissed as irrelevant.

There is already considerable evidence to indicate that the real prophets of today are outside the church. One of the 1959 Earl Lecturers at the Pacific School of Religion was not a theologian or a churchman in the professional sense, but the editor of a secular magazine. It was natural and right that Norman Cousins of *The Saturday Review* should have been invited for this distinguished lectureship. For several years now, ministers of every denomination have been finding in his editorials the prophetic utterances they wish they had been the first to pronounce. It's a new day when ministers look to a secular journalist for their inspiration.

And Norman Cousins is not the only one to give this kind of guidance. In Little Rock, while progressive church leaders were not entirely silent, the *Arkansas Gazette* seems to have seized the moral initiative and provided the leadership for the forces of decency and order that normally would be expected from the churches. Attempts to reduce the circulation of the paper and to organize the advertisers to boycott it did not intimidate J. N. Heiskell, president and editor, or Harry Ashmore, the executive editor. Under threats, they did not pull their punches. Writing the story of the Gazette and its two Pulitzer prizes—one to the paper itself, and one to its executive editor—Bruce Catton observes, "The *Arkansas Gazette* happens to be the oldest newspaper west of the Mississippi River. It was established in 1819, and in the ordinary course of things it might be expected to be so deeply crusted with age and tradition that it would play everything safe, editorialize only on subjects that never reached the level of live controversy, and cuddle up to its readers, its advertisers and the powers-that-be in the hope of enjoying an untroubled and prosperous senescence." In actual practice, however, the editors gambled their professional (and even physical) lives on the conviction that they had a moral responsibility to report the facts as they saw them, to expose the acts and intentions of selfishly-motivated men, and to stand firmly for law and order.

Not all preachers are equally courageous. With a few slight changes to make the words apply to the clergy rather than to editors, Bruce Catton's description of how things might have been with the *Gazette* tells the story of too many ministers: "They play everything safe, preach only on subjects that never reach the level of live controversy, and cuddle up to their members, their boards, and the powers-that-be in the hope of enjoying an untroubled and prosperous senescence."

The journalists, however, are not the only ones who have slipped the torch of idealism from the hands of the clergy in order to hold it a little higher. Many distinguished statesmen have done the same. The members of the Supreme Court are one example. Elsewhere in the world are men like Nehru, who doesn't even claim to be a Christian, but who repeatedly beckons men to higher standards, more in keeping with God's purpose.

The point is that when we ministers are afraid to touch controversial issues, we are in danger of surrending our rightful place of leadership in the community and in the world to men who are not afraid. James Robinson goes to the heart of the matter when he says, "Most Christians hold politicians in contempt, or merely tolerate them. Politicians, however, often influence our government and its legislation far more significantly than all ministers, priests, and rabbis taken together." So it becomes increasingly evident that ministers who are more concerned with avoiding controversy than with discovering the truth and preaching it are traitors to the church. The world will follow the leader with bold ideas and the courage to affirm them, and if such leaders are not found in the church, history will walk off and leave it. To the extent that any of us have hedged and hesitated, toned down and modified the message God has given us to speak, we have weakened the church and betrayed our high calling. And in varying degrees, most of us are guilty.

The second characteristic ministers tend to develop when they face the dilemma of a radical message in a conservative society is a contentious spirit. Like the extreme social-action men, they are always crusading and they are always opposing. Overconfident that they have the complete answer to the complex social problems of the world, they confront church bodies with the necessity of declaring themselves at once on specific issues. Any move to postpone action to give time for more careful study they interpret as cowardice, and they are quick to brand a man as a reactionary if he doesn't jump on their band wagon. They always anticipate a fight and usually get it. Entering the ring swinging, sooner or later they pop somebody, and the conflict they knew they would have is under way.

I have always considered myself a social liberal, but more than once I have been embarrassed by fellow ministers whose basic social philosophy I accept, but whose method of winning other people to it I reject. I have never considered it an act of compromise to go slow enough to be convincing; and I have never been impressed with the notion that you win people to your point of view by forcing them prematurely to take sides. There have been times when ardent reformers have driven me right out of their camp and into the arms of the conservatives by insisting that I take a more extreme stand than I was ready to take.

There is no doubt that someone needs to arouse the social conscience of Christians, but I have long been convinced that extremists have the opposite effect. They arouse something all right, but it isn't a social conscience; it's personal antipathy. I am more in accord with the attitude of the policeman who took a friend and me to church one Sunday morning in Kansas City. When we stopped to ask him for directions, he offered to deliver us to the church door in style and on the city's gasoline. On the way he filled us in on the nature of a policeman's usual Sunday chores: settling family rows. One day when he went to the address where a wife had called for help, she was waiting for him at the door. "Who called?" he asked. "I did," she said, and pointing inside where her drunken, belligerent husband was to be found, she added, "He's in there." "What do you want me to do," asked the policeman, "run him in?" "No," she said, "just go in and give him a good scare." "Lady," said the policeman firmly, "I know I'm ugly but my job isn't to scare people."

We ministers can take a leaf from his notebook. Our job isn't to scare people, nor to antagonize them—although honest preaching will sometimes have that result. Our job is to win them. We must never forget that.

Undoubtedly ministers who are unnecessarily zealous about social reform are compensating in this manner for some deep-seated personality problems. The true Christian minister knows that he does not have to go out looking for issues and he doesn't have to excite antagonism. The issues will find him, and sooner or later he will be involved in a battle he didn't ask for, but which he cannot avoid.

This brings us to the third characteristic ministers develop in the face of controversial issues: responsible Christian leadership. Men of this type know that the question of being liberal or conservative, radical or reactionary, is beside the point. Their job is to know and speak the truth, to discover the will of God and do it. If this causes the radicals to call them reactionaries, and the reactionaries to call them radicals, let it be so. The silly efforts of little men to classify everyone are not for them. They do not arouse antagonism unnecessarily, but they are not afraid to antagonize. They know there is a time to speak up and a time to remain silent. Not the first to champion a cause, they are its sturdiest supporters when it is seen to be sound.

People of this type have more than conviction. They have skill in human relations. Benjamin Franklin, although inclined in his early years to be argumentative, learned that a less direct approach was more likely to gain him his ends. He made it a point, when dealing with a controversial issue, never to use the words "certainly," or "undoubtedly," or other too-positive assertions. Rather he would say, "I conceive or apprehend a thing to be so and so; it appears to me, or I should think it so or so, for such and such reasons; or I imagine it to be so; or it is so, if I am not mistaken. And he adds:

This habit, I believe, has been of great advantage to me when I have had occasion to inculcate my opinions, and persuade men into measures that I have been from time to time engag'd in promoting. . . . I wish well-meaning, sensible men would not lessen their power of doing good by a positive, assuming manner, that seldom fails to disgust, tends to create opposition, and to defeat everyone of those purposes for which speech was given to us. . . . For, if you would inform, a positive and dogmatical manner in advancing your sentiments may provoke contradiction and prevent a candid attention. If you wish information and improvement from the knowledge of others, and yet at the same time express yourself as firmly fix'd in your present opinions, modest, sensible men, who do not love disputation, will probably leave you undisturbed in the possession of your error. And by such a manner, you can seldom hope to recommend yourself in pleasing your hearers, or to persuade those whose concurrence you desire. Pope says, judiciously:

> "Men should be taught as if you taught them not,
> And things unknown propos'd as things forgot";

farther recommending to us

> "To speak, tho' sure with seeming diffidence."[1]

Perhaps ours is a day more friendly to direct speech and candid expression of views, but human nature remains much the same. The average person is still more readily won to a new idea by being wooed than by being badgered.

It must be noted, however, that the minister who tries to be pleasant about his "radicalism" always runs the risk of growing more and more pleasant and less and less radical. The more one allows his heated concern to cool, the less likely he is to do anything about it. In William J. Lederer and Eugene Burdick's *The Ugly American*, one chapter describes how Tom Knox was confronted with this very problem. Tom was a chicken expert from America, working with the people of Cambodia, in southeast Asia. He knew and understood the people better than anyone else in the diplomatic service. And he knew how American aid money could best be used. But he was an "American Junior Grade," and his excellent ideas were vetoed by men with more power but less sense. This infuriated Tom and he resigned from his post to return to the United States, go straight to Washington, and tell them the truth. However, it was cleverly arranged that, out of appreciation for his fine service, he would be given a special trip en route home. Rather than flying directly back across the Pacific, he would be given an opportunity to visit "the rest of the Far Eastern countries, India, the Middle East, and France and England."

The trip was delightful. He traveled first class, and every courtesy was extended to him wherever he went. And the longer he traveled, the less Cambodia and its problems seemed to matter. Finally, two days out of New York, he sat down in his luxury suite on the *Liberté* and began to write down his ideas and plan his strategy for presenting the facts to congressional committees and newspaper men. But the authors make this significant statement:

He discovered, however, that not only had his feeling of anger and outrage been blunted, but that it was very difficult to recreate it at all. To his astonishment Cambodia seemed a long, long time away, and glazed over with wonderful memories. These were not so much memories of the village life, as of the generous and courteous attentions he had been given by so many Cambodians on his trip home. The anger, which in Cambodia had seemed so sure and honest a weapon, in his suite on the *Liberté* seemed somehow almost ridiculous. After working for three hours and covering only a half a page, he resolved to wait until he had landed.

Eight months later, when Tom was back on the Knox farm in Sheldon, Iowa, he again saw the half page of paper. When he read it over, he thought for a moment that it must have been written by another person. The handwriting was his, but not the words. The anger he had felt in Cambodia, so hot and bright and curiously nourishing, now seemed childish. Tom folded the paper and put it away.[2]

Many needed reforms have died in that manner, and more than one worthy cause has lost a potential champion in just that way. Ministers have to be constantly on their guard if they are not to lose their passion for social concerns through the courtesies of the gracious but privileged people in their congregations. Social reform and social courtesy are sometimes hard to mix, but the minister has the difficult role of seeing that one never crowds out the other.

The minister who is a responsible Christian leader is seldom a self-conscious reformer. He doesn't get embroiled in disputes because of his love of controversy, but because of his devotion to the Christian gospel. He doesn't follow Christ's way because it leads to conflict; but when it leads to conflict, he still follows it.

Few ministers have been the focal point of more bitter denunciation or the center of more heated debate than Harry Emerson Fosdick at the time of the famed fundamentalist controversy. But through it all, this great preacher never lost his perspective. As he put it, "I went on trying to saw wood." He admits that "preaching Sunday after Sunday amid such angry denunciations was not easy," but says, "I did my best not to let the controversy dominate my ministry or make me forget what preaching was really meant to accomplish." He was particularly grateful for a statement Charles Clayton Morrison wrote about him in the *Christian Century*. He said, "What I like most about Fosdick the heretic is that he does not seem to care about capitalizing his heresy. He keeps capitalizing his catholicity, just as if he were an unnoted and humble pastor directly responsible for the souls of the modest flock which the Father had given him to tend." And Fosdick concludes, "That, at any rate, was what I tried to do, although of course I was blasted for *that* by radicals who wanted me to shout shocking heresies every Sunday."[3]

In more recent days, Martin Luther King, Jr., has found himself at the center of a reform movement. Like Fosdick, he did not ask to play the leading role and he did not reject it when it came. He, too, was ruthlessly condemned by the reactionaries; more than once his life was threatened. And on the other side, hotheaded radicals would have had him push faster, harder, and more violently. But, a true minister of Jesus Christ, he was intent only upon discovering God's will and fulfilling it.

This is the life all of us must lead. It is the challenge we accepted when we entered the ministry. And, more than some people realize, our laymen support us when we live and preach this way. When I asked a group of fifteen or twenty of my leading laymen what role they wanted their minister to play at the time of a national election, they were unanimous in the opinion that a minister not only should feel free to show his political colors, but that he had a responsibility to do so. It was their conviction that people are looking for leadership in these crucial matters, and it helps them to make decisions if they know where their minister stands.

Recently J. Stanford Smith, a Methodist layman who is manager of public and employee relations services of the General Electric Company in New York City, wrote a stimulating article entitled "What the Layman Expects of His Minister." It appeared in *The New Christian Advocate*. He said, "I think the layman has a right to expect moral and ethical leadership from his minister. I well realize that the charge is often made that laymen don't want such moral leadership but want the preacher to confirm their prejudices, to endorse the *status quo*, and to say only the things that he knows they would like to hear from him.

"I don't believe it. I don't believe that the average layman has respect for a reed swaying in the wind; rather he is looking for a minister who truly stands for something, knows what he stands for, and does not hesitate to speak out for it."[4]

So if we ministers are to rise to the expectations of the best laymen in our churches and stand in the tradition of the prophets, we must be clear about what the issues of this generation are, and we must affirm a positive position in connection with them. Which ones we concentrate upon, and exactly what we say or do about them, may depend upon the location of our parish and the needs of the people in our church. But in any event we cannot remain silent in the face of social injustice or international suicide.

One of the crucial questions has to do with race relations. I cannot imagine a section of the world today so remote from society's struggles as to excuse a minister serving there from dealing squarely with this issue. Human survival may hinge on our solution to the race problem. Certainly America's claim to world leadership is bound up with it. By clear implication the Christian gospel has some forthright things to say about race relations; and most of our denominational bodies have spoken specifically on the subject. We must talk about desegregation in the public schools, open housing, intermarriage, and integrated churches.

Specific action will vary from place to place, but the motivating Christian principle is the same. While one minister is integrating his congregation, another is assuring his that the sky will not tumble if their children meet youngsters of other races in the classrooms at school. In one section of the country it may be a great advance to get Negro and white ministerial associations to meet together, while in another section, the progressive step is to put Negro, white, and Oriental ministers on the staff of the same church. No man can tell another what his action should be; each must get his orders from God. One thing, however, seems certain: if the step one takes is easy, it probably isn't enough. Time is running out on us, and we must proceed toward full human brotherhood with utmost speed.

A second issue no preacher can sidestep is communism. We have to do more than condemn it. We must define it, and we must wrestle with it. The most constructive thing that could happen to many of us would be to be thrust into direct contact with a bona fide Communist, and learn for ourselves that he is a real human being who thinks he has the answer to humanity's ills. We must face the fact that most of our people have only the foggiest notion of what communism is, and they wouldn't recognize a devotee of Marx if they saw one. Some know so little about the characteristics of a Communist that they can't distinguish between a Christian with a sense of social justice and a fellow traveler. At the very least, we who are Christian ministers must help our people to recognize a Communist when they see one, and know when a man is being falsely accused. Beyond this minimum requirement, progressive churches may plan study tours of Russia, encourage their youth to learn the Russian language, and prepare in every way possible for a face-to-face grappling of ideas between Communists and Christians.

A third issue to be met head on is social drinking and alcoholism. This is often difficult to deal with. There are few if any Communists in our churches, but there are a good many people who drink, some of them to excess. So the problem is often acutely personal. The whole matter is further complicated by the fact that, in the past, the church has spawned some unattractive reformers in this area. When most people hear that a "temperance man" is to visit the church, they expect a crank. Consequently, we are inclined to be timid about dealing with this matter. We don't want people to think we are odd. But in this issue as in others, we must not be afraid to be radical. It is sometimes necessary to be "fools" for Christ's sake.

Another controversial issue that the pulpit should tangle with is militarism and war. With power for total destruction concentrated on opposite sides of the globe, and deadly missiles pointed at the cities in which we live, this is a subject of extreme relevance. In early American villages, the town's supply of powder and balls was often kept in the churches. Ready for "instant retaliation," it was conveniently placed under lock and key directly under the pulpit. In the mid-twentieth century, the powder may not rest under the preacher's feet, but the threat of destruction hangs over our heads. Never was it more appropriate to counsel the preacher to preach "as a dying man to dying men." The Christian gospel has something to say about a way of life that spends its resources on ever deadlier means of destruction while children starve and men's souls shrivel; and we preachers must say it. In *The Causes of World War Three*, C. Wright Mills says challengingly that "two groups are especially relevant, even strategic, to stopping the thrust toward World War III and getting on the road to peace: ministers of God and physical scientists." But he doesn't have much faith that the ministers will meet the challenge. In a chapter entitled "A Pagan Sermon," he says to the clergy:

In moral affairs you are supposed to be among the first of men. No moral affair today compares with the morality of warfare and the preparation for it, for in these preparations men usurp—as you might say—the prerogatives of God. By sitting down and by keeping quiet, by all too often echoing the claptrap of the higher immorality that now passes for political leadership, you are helping to enfeeble further in this time of cruel troubles the ideals of your founder.[5]

That is straight talk about what preachers might do. It is our business to see that they don't.

There are many other crucial controversial issues which we must not avoid in our preaching, but which cannot be included here in any detail. Here are some of them: Roman Catholicism and American freedom; birth control, and getting the lid on the population explosion; labor vs. management; corruption in the labor unions; education for science; American foreign policy. The reader can think of more, but perhaps enough have been mentioned to give the homiletical mill a good start. Let us bring our fear of being radical under control, whip up our courage, and preach the whole gospel. As we fulfill with graciousness our role as priest, let us not neglect our role as prophet. Let even the children perceive the sternness in the word of God.

But let us never forget that we are a part of the society we seek to reform. We can speak the word of God but we can't assume the role of God. One evening toward the close of World War II, our small son climbed up in his mother's lap and asked thoughtfully, "Mommy, why do people fly planes that drop bombs that kill people?" She answered as best she could, but he continued his questions: "Is it wrong to fly planes that drop bombs that kill people?" "Yes," she said, "it is wrong." Then the little fellow asked, "Did your brother fly a plane that dropped bombs that killed people?" My wife says that she has never found it harder to answer a child's question. Yes, her brother did pilot a bomber, and we helped pay for it and put it in the air. We are all involved in the sins of society. Mellowed by an awareness of this, the preacher's message should not be less prophetic, but more persuasive.

X

THE RIGHT THING AT THE RIGHT TIME

❖ ❖ ❖

How insecure I felt the first time I conducted a funeral service! How long should I talk? What should I say about the deceased? Where should I stand? Where should I be and what should I be doing while people were "viewing the remains"? No one helped me much with these matters. The undertaker was relaxed enough about his own responsibilities, and didn't seem to understand why I should have any questions. "Do whatever you want," he said. Ministers whom I had consulted had given me a few hints, but no one seemed to appreciate how many uncertainties remained in my mind.

There are many questions a young man entering the ministry has about what is the proper thing to do. Sometimes a course in seminary fills him in on these matters, but most men are left to get them the way children used to get information about the birds and the bees. They just picked it up here and there. Often, however, the questions continue through life, and a man never does feel entirely at home in certain situations.

So we are devoting this chapter, not to any one tension in the minister's life, but to all those little strains that come from not knowing what is the right or correct thing to do. I suspect that if inner tension could be measured, these little strains would add up to a rather impressive total.

Of course there are wide individual differences. Some men

are less self-conscious than others, and less afraid of making a mistake. Backgrounds vary. There are men who enter the ministry from homes and communities that have taught them few of the social graces. Even so seemingly simple a gesture as introducing one person to another is an act performed with hesitancy and embarrassment. Others, however, seem to know instinctively how to behave in each social situation.

The problem is further complicated for some as they are transferred from one type of church and community to another. The average layman learns what stratum of society he feels most comfortable with, and quickly finds his element when he moves from one section of the country to another. The minister, however, may be transferred from a small rural church to a fashionable suburban one. He may minister in one church that serves "navy families" or "labor families," and another that draws its membership from professional people and the town's leading citizens. He is expected to feel equally at home with all of them.

Now there are a few general rules that can guide the minister through all of these circumstances. They can be stated briefly. After that we'll go into more detail about some specifics.

The first rule is to be kind. The best etiquette centers in consideration of others. If a man is more concerned with helping the other person to feel at ease than with feeling at ease himself, he may accomplish the job for both. A person who loves other people and is basically thoughtful is an honored guest in any company. This isn't to say that if one has a good heart he can forget about matters of propriety. On the contrary, his very concern for other people dictates that he observe the social amenities, if for no other reason than to avoid embarrassing a host or humiliating a guest.

The second rule is to be natural. Stiffness and awkwardness are never in order. This, of course, is a difficult rule to apply. Telling a person who is ill at ease to be natural is like telling a nervous person to relax, or an anxious soul to stop worrying. There is nothing the victim would like more than to follow the advice. The question is how? This is something we all have to work at. Naturalness comes with self-confidence. Self-confidence is grounded in humility. Humility is a Christian grace we all seek to win. I think as a general rule most ministers become more natural as they grow older. This is especially true if they have had a measure of success and no longer need to strive to impress people. It sometimes helps to remind oneself that it doesn't really matter much what other people think of him. He isn't responsible for their reactions. It is more important what he thinks of them. And most important of all is what he and God think of each other.

The third rule is to get a good book on social etiquette and read it. One should also read the code of ministerial ethics for his denomination.[1] People are prone to stumble along feeling inadequate in normal social gatherings because they aren't sure of the correct thing to do, when the answer is as near as the library.

Beyond these general rules there are some things to be said that may be helpful to ministers faced with the specific problems of the profession. For example, most ministers are a little uncertain about their relations with the laymen of a church they have left. And they are sometimes strained in their relations with a predecessor or successor. Often men who have been the best of friends become cool toward each other when one succeeds the other as pastor of a church. Happily, the reverse of this is also sometimes true, and men drawn together through the predecessor-successor relationship deepen their friendship.

It is important for a man to remember that when he has left a church he is no longer the pastor of the people in it. A new man is in charge. In all probability he will employ different methods of church administration; his pastoral manner will not be like his predecessor's; his wife will follow a pattern of

behavior quite different from that of the previous minister's
wife. But none of this is the business of the man who has left.
He has no claim whatsoever on the church he previously
served.

But all of this is easier to say than to live up to. The man
who has "meddled" in the affairs of his previous church has
come in for his full share of condemnation, but he has not
always been understood. There is no question but that there
have been men who have caused no end of trouble by returning to a former parish to take weddings or funerals, or to
give counsel to the laymen. Sometimes they deliberately foster
dissatisfaction with the new man. This is unethical, and any
man stooping to such behavior should be disciplined. But it
is also true that there have been men coming into a church
who have shown no respect whatsoever for their predecessor.
Sometimes they are openly critical of everything he did, and
tell the laymen how wrong it was. Sometimes they restrain
themselves from such open opposition, but quickly change
everything their predecessor had set up, not bothering to live
with it long enough to see whether or not it had any values.
They behave like a woman married to a widower who quickly
clears the house of everything that might evoke the memory of
his previous wife. All of this is frankly insulting, but little has
been said or written about it. It seems quite clear, however,
that if it is unethical for a man to continue to bring direct influence upon the life of a church he no longer serves, it is
equally unethical for a minister, either directly or by inference,
to cast reflection upon his predecessor. It is often said that
certain men are hard to succeed. Some men are also hard to
precede.

Two things in particular make the predecessor role a hard
one to play. The first is the minister's own emotional involvement in the church he has served. If he has been there for
several years, and has been a good preacher and faithful pastor,
his life is interwoven with the lives of his people, and the

fabric is not easily severed. If he has been a true minister, he has come to love his church and the people in it. Perhaps it was under his leadership that the building was constructed. The pulpit was built exactly to his liking, and the educational plant is his dream come true. Through many a long meeting he has guided his people to the fulfillment of the ideals they shaped up together. He has baptized the babies that have grown now into their youth; he has seen families through their sorrow, and steadied them when they were faced with major crises. After all of this, it is a good deal to expect of a man that he should drop these relationships as though they had never been. Most of us cannot even move from a house we have loved without a pang of sorrow when we close the door on it for the last time. It is harder yet to close the door on meaningful human relations. This is especially difficult if one feels somewhat a stranger in his new church and contemplates the fact that the deep friendships he had in his former parish took a long time to grow.

A second thing that makes the predecessor role difficult is the attitude of the laymen. Some of them will find it hard to adjust to their new minister, and will be quick to tell the former man all of the "mistakes" that are being made. "We still think of you as our pastor," they will begin flatteringly. This is a personal compliment he hesitates to reject. Besides, it's obviously true. Or the layman may say, "We tried to follow your advice and give the new man the same loyalty we gave to you. But it won't work." Then there follows a long list of grievances.

What is the minister to say? Shall he listen but make no response? That isn't easy. Shall he cut them off short and say bluntly—if somewhat artificially—that he refuses to listen to any criticism of his successor? But they mean no offense, and they need to unburden themselves. Shall he say of his successor, "Oh, he's a great guy. You'll like him fine when you get used to him." But what if he doesn't believe that? Shall he refuse to answer mail that comes from his previous parishioners? And shall he frankly discourage them from telephoning or visiting him? It hardly seems appropriate for a Christian minister to refuse to see people, or to listen to their troubles.

The truth is that the adjustment from one minister to another may prove to be a traumatic experience in the life of the laymen. You see, they have tensions too, and one of them is the struggle to extend to a minister the same loyalty and support they gave his predecessor. I often marvel at the ability of most laymen to adjust to the idiosyncrasies of a succession of preachers, but I hope I never presume upon it. Ministers sometimes complain about their recalcitrant laymen; but, generally speaking, ministers are as set in their ways as their parishioners are.

However, a wise clergyman will seek to put himself in his laymen's shoes. He will understand that his appearance on the scene is a bitter pill for some people to take, and he will sympathize with them in their apprehension lest "the new man" should want to change everything they have come to love and feel comfortable with. That may be exactly what he intends to do, but at least for his own sake, if not for theirs, he should win their affection before shaking up their environment too drastically. When they come to love him they will make the changes much faster, and they will be happy in the bargain. What is more, they will not feel compelled to run to their former minister for comfort.

Well, how is this predecessor-successor business best handled? Probably not by rules. Rules become arbitrary, and people become fussy if they are not followed to the letter. Often they create more tension than they dissolve, and they are usually hardest on the conscientious. If you want a fairly specific guide, perhaps these lines from "The Disciples Code" will be helpful:

I will refrain from speaking disparagingly about the work of either my predecessor or my successor.

I will refrain from frequent visits to a former field and if, in exceptional cases, I am called back for a funeral or wedding, I will request that the resident minister be invited to participate in the service.

I will never embarrass my successor by meddling in the affairs of the church I formerly served.

I will be courteous to any predecessor of mine when he returns to the field, and will be thoughtful of any retired minister.

In the finest of relationships a predecessor should be proud of his successor and enthusiastic about the work he is doing; and a successor should be eager to have his predecessor drop around, knowing that he will strengthen and undergird him. Normally, when a change is made, the new man should have a talk with his predecessor to ask him questions about his dreams for the church, what he thinks the next steps should be, who is to be depended upon, and of whom he should beware. A wise predecessor will not take advantage of such an interview to vent his prejudices, or seek to determine what the future program should be. But it is inconceivable that a man who has been in a church for five, ten, or twenty years does not have some valuable information and insight he can pass along to the next man. After that the new man should be completely free to follow his own wisdom without the slightest fear that his predecessor will be disturbed if he makes drastic changes. Besides, the predecessor should keep in mind that the very appearance of the new man on the scene has changed the church greatly, and his old plans and ways of doing things may no longer be applicable.

In most instances, a wise minister will also invite his predecessor to return to preach at an early date. Failure to do this suggests either that he is jealous of him, mistrusts him, or has no respect for him. The invitation may or may not be accepted. But in any event the congregation has the reassurance of know-

ing that there is no animosity between the two ministers, and
the position of the man currently on the job is greatly strengthened. Also, an open invitation to return to the parish keeps
everything above board so that neither the predecessor nor the
laymen feel that any contacts must be secretive lest the present
minister be upset.

In the last analysis the whole relationship must be based on
good sense and Christian love. It should be quite clear that a
man who has left a church is no longer pastor to the people
there. But it should be equally clear that he is their friend, and
the normal associations of friendship should be continued
without hindrance or embarrassment. Naturally it is to be supposed that an active minister is much too busy wherever he is
to spend much time in the company of former parishioners. A
smart predecessor will bend over backward to stay away from
his former parish unless he is invited by the minister. And he
will not stand around waiting for the invitation or complaining
if it doesn't come. A smart successor, on the other hand, will
be quick to assure his predecessor of a cordial welcome, and to
create special opportunities for him to return to the church.
And smart laymen will continue their friendship with their
former minister; quite naturally they will fill him in on how
things are going at the church, but they will tell the good as
well as the bad, and they will never put him in the position of
adviser on church affairs. If they have real complaints, they
will take them to the properly appointed church boards or
officials, but never involve their former minister even by
implication. And they will always turn to their present minister
for all pastoral services such as weddings, funerals, baptisms,
or calling and counseling.

Another set of problems centers around weddings and
funerals. Here again a sincere minister wants to do the right
thing at the right time, but he is often uncertain what that is.

Take the matter of fees, for example. It is generally understood that a minister never accepts gratuities from the mem-

bers of his congregation or their families. When he officiates at a funeral or a wedding for one of them, he is merely doing the job for which he is paid. They are to expect that service just because they are a part of the church fellowship.

That all sounds simple enough, but in actual practice it is often confusing and sometimes embarrassing. For one thing, families who are served at these crucial periods of their lives frequently feel a deep indebtedness to their pastor. He has come to be very close to them and they want to express their gratitude and affection in some tangible way. What we so commercially call a fee is to them a love gift. It is a direct rebuff, therefore, when the minister lifts his hand like a police officer stopping traffic, and says, "I never accept fees from the members of my church." They hadn't been thinking of it that way. If they had, they probably would have reached into their pocket, pulled out a $10 bill and handed it to the parson just as they would pay the cashier at the grocery store. But they have written out a check, or gone to the trouble of getting a crisp new bill and put it in an envelope with a note of appreciation. Is it entirely gracious for the minister to turn that down?

In the case of funerals there is often another complication. Usually the ministerial fee is figured into the total cost of the funeral service, and the minister receives his check directly from the mortician. How should he handle this? Should he accept the check and endorse it over to the family? Should he refuse to accept it and let the undertaker make the adjustment with the family? Or should he just accept it the way he does his salary check and say nothing more about it? I have heard men complain that when they have left the matter to the undertaker they are never sure the family has been reimbursed or that it has been explained to them that the minister refused to accept anything for his services.

Recently I asked a mature minister, who has been at this business a long while and has been an attentive pastor, how he handled the problem. "What do you do," I asked, "when church members offer you a fee for weddings or funerals?" "I accept it," he said. He went on to explain that he had worried about this problem for some time, but finally came to the conclusion that he was doing a greater kindness to his people by allowing them to express their appreciation this way than by blocking their impulse to do so. This same man refused a raise in salary when it was offered. It is very evident he does not accept the fees because he wants the money, but because he believes it is the best way to serve the people.

Another friend goes to the opposite extreme. Not only does he refuse to accept fees from members; he refuses to accept any fees at all. He does not want people to feel that spiritual services are for sale. If the question comes up with a couple he has married, for example, he tells them to go to church next Sunday and place their love offering on the collection plate.

It is difficult, and probably unwise, to establish a rule in this matter. Rules are brittle. People are not. It is much easier to solve the problem once and for all by one clear-cut regulation, but probably it is more in line with the calling of a true pastor to adapt to the circumstances and seek to do the thing that is best for the people involved in each situation. The statements on this matter in the denominational codes might be helpful guides. The Congregationalists say, "The minister recognizes himself to be the servant of the community in which he resides. Fees which are offered should be accepted only in the light of this principle." The Disciples are brief: "I will not seek special gratuities." And the Unitarians say, "Professional service should be gladly rendered to all, without regard to compensation, except for necessary expenses incurred."

The place where weddings or funeral services are to be held is another question that sometimes worries the preacher. Most funeral directors are not eager to move their base of operations to the church. It is an inconvenience to them, especially if they are running a tight schedule on funerals. Their convenience should be considered, and their good will solicited. Some ministers do not recognize this. Generally opposed to a business that profits from human sorrow, and displeased with the eagerness of morticians to display their art, some of them rather like to make things difficult for the undertakers just to prove the church is still in the business. This, of course, is unministerial. However, in the case of families who want a funeral from the church, especially if the deceased has been an active churchman, the minister should work co-operatively with the undertakers to see that the family's wishes are honored.

The location of weddings is often a greater problem. People can come up with some bizarre ideas. Occasionally a couple want to be married in an airplane. Often they prefer private homes, gardens, or the minister's study to the church sanctuary or chapel. One couple recently asked Dr. Goozee on my church staff to marry them under an arch at the head of Lake Merritt in downtown Oakland. The particular location is where heavy traffic streams by at all hours of the day. After consultation, they were happily married at church.

Here again, it is of paramount importance to understand the people you are working with and to do the thing which is best for their development. It should be remembered that a wedding conducted by a minister is a worship service, and couples selecting a location for their wedding should be encouraged to choose a place most suitable for a worship experience.

This assumes that there is consultation in advance. And around this question more ministerial tensions accumulate. Some ministers make a great deal of the importance of this, especially in connection with weddings, but to a certain extent with funerals also. There are those who will not marry a couple except after a series of consultations. The meaning of marriage and the couple's readiness for the experience are discussed with care and every detail of the wedding is gone into. Additional help is given at the rehearsal and in planning for the reception. If a minister wants to use his time this way, I have no objection to it. Certainly young people should be given every assistance in getting their marriage off to a good start. More and more, however, I have come to see premarital testing and counseling as a specialized field. It is time-consuming, and if a minister is located where he is likely to have many weddings, a major portion of his time could be used in this one phase of the ministry. For me it seems more sensible to have one consultation to size up the general maturity of the couple and to check details. If further counseling is required, the couple can be referred to specialists in the field; or if none are available, the minister may want to give them additional time himself.

As for questions of etiquette in connection with the wedding and reception, a church should have a wedding hostess, employed or volunteer, who counsels with the couple on these matters. Certainly a minister does not want to use his time this way. Where a church has a secretary, she can easily take care of business arrangements concerning use of rooms, custodial and music fees, and similar matters. This frees the minister to spend all of his time with the couple dealing with marriage itself and the personalities of the people entering into it.

The same kind of consultation is not necessary in connection with funerals, but families should be seen in advance of the service. Some men are bold to say they know what a funeral service should be like, and solicit no suggestions from the family. As for myself, however, I like to give people a chance to suggest a favorite scripture or bit of poetry they would like to have used. If it seems unsuitable, they can usually be led to substitute something more appropriate. I have also found it helpful to encourage the family to talk about the one they have lost. Not only is this a therapeutic experience for them, but it helps me to catch more of the personality of the one in whose honor and memory the service is being held.

One can go too far, however, in the direction of letting others influence the services at which he officiates. I once was requested to delete any mention of God from the wedding ceremony. Sometimes enthusiastic youth can get carried away with the idea of writing their own wedding service. Seldom do they improve on the ritual!

One of the hardest things to handle is the participation of other parties in the service. Sometimes a couple feel close to several ministers and want them all to take part. It is not always easy to include them and still retain the basic unity and orderliness which give dignity and beauty to the service. But these accommodations have to be worked out with good grace. Much less pleasant is to share a funeral service with a lodge! The church has a complete ritual for the burial of the dead. So do most lodges. Why some people insist on having both, I suspect I'll go to my own funeral wondering. Even if the two are not contradictory in mood and emphasis, which they often are, at least they were designed to be complete in themselves and neither has any room for the other. I once heard a Methodist Bishop say that he had come to the place where he refused to take a funeral if a lodge was to participate. I have never felt justified in establishing such a policy, but I often wish I had. If ministers could get together on the matter, perhaps they could encourage funeral directors to persuade people to make up their minds which they want, a church funeral or a lodge funeral, and select one or the other, but not both. If they insist on both, the least that could be done would be to have one take the service at the funeral parlor and the other at the graveside. My own conviction is that a practicing Christian should ask to be buried through the good services of the church. If his lodge wishes to commemorate him, let it hold a memorial service at its own meeting place a week or two later.

Where a church has a multiple staff, another problem often appears. A senior minister may monopolize the funeral and wedding business, denying other ministers a chance to have the experience. Of course, he is at once suspected of having an eye on the gratuities involved. However, there is another element. In their choice of a parson to officiate at a wedding or funeral, people are casting a kind of popularity vote. Some men are very sensitive to this, and keep careful score. Staff tensions often develop at this point.

There are various ways in which this can be handled. One is to make certain designations of days of the week when men are or are not available to take weddings or funerals. Another is to designate one minister on the staff to take all but exceptional situations. A "Minister of the Parish," for example, might be expected to handle most of the funerals. Another possibility is to put the whole matter on an individual basis, encouraging people to select whichever minister they wish to have. Many factors will condition their selection. Some people are likely to choose the senior minister just because he is the senior minister and they think of anyone else as a substitute for him. It is unfortunate that they feel that way, but until they become more accustomed to a multiple ministry and the qualifications of each member of the staff, this notion will dominate. Staff personnel must learn to accept this fact without resentment. Other people will select the minister they have been working with most closely. A popular minister in charge of youth work, for example, is likely to be asked by the people he works with to officiate at their weddings. And a good Minister of the Parish who has been calling regularly on a member during a long illness can be expected to be invited to take over the funeral when death finally comes.

Many other questions face the minister in connection with what to do and when to do it. Actually practices vary in different parts of the country and in different communions. I do not pretend to have the authoritative answers to any of these matters, but in the interest of brevity let me employ a simple question-and-answer method to tell what I think should be done about some of them.

1. Should a minister join a service club?

This strikes me as an individual matter. It depends somewhat on whether a man enjoys that kind of activity or not, and what kind of service clubs are available. Once when I asked a leading clergyman whether or not he was active in a service club, he said he had tried most of them—Lions, Kiwanis, and the rest—but currently belonged to none. He didn't have time to bother with them. Another man testifies that through most of his ministry he avoided service clubs, believing they were a waste of time, and then finally broke down and joined. He was surprised to learn that he enjoyed the contacts and was stimulated by the experience. If a church expects its minister to belong to a service club, then the church should pick up the tab.

2. Is it proper to accept a pastoral responsibility in another man's parish?

For a variety of reasons men are sometimes asked to take a wedding or funeral or render other pastoral assistance to members of another church. Normally this should be no cause for alarm. The total number of people "stolen" from another parish must be very small. Most people are loyal to their own church even when you can't see what there is there to make them stay. However, just to keep the record straight, a man should give his brother pastor a call on the telephone to let him know the circumstances which seem to make it wise to reach over into his field. Often the two men can work together on the situation. It should be assumed that both are interested more in rendering the proper pastoral service to the persons involved than in their own prerogatives.

3. Should visiting ministers be called on to participate in the Sunday service, or should attention be called to their presence in the congregation?

It depends somewhat on who the visitor is and what church he is visiting. In small churches where the service is informal and where ministers are seldom seen in the congregation, it would not be out of order to mention the presence of the visitor. He should not be called on to take part in the service, however, unless the matter has been cleared in advance. Once when I was worshiping in another church, the minister introduced the prayer by saying, "Let us bow in prayer. Reverend Walker will lead us." That was my first notice! Another time, when a minister approached me before the service, asking if I would lead in prayer, I declined, explaining that I so rarely had the opportunity to sit through a service with my family that I should prefer to be just another worshiper. I thought the matter was agreed, but after the service began, he announced my presence in the congregation and asked me to come to the platform and lead in the morning prayer. I am sure he did not think he was offending me. He was a gentleman. Probably he thought I was just being modest in what I had said before, and really would like a chance to participate.

Most of the men I talk with about this matter agree that they have all the spotlight they need, and when they slip into another man's congregation they prefer not to be singled out. However, there are some exceptions. When a particularly distinguished churchman is in the audience, the minister may want to mention this. If he is an executive of the denomination, or someone else whom the church people ought to know, he might be invited to stand with the minister to greet worshipers at the close of the service.

4. Should a minister permit other ministers to use his church for weddings or other services?

Of course. If some specific problem develops, it can be handled on its own merits.

5. Is it expected that a minister make a pastoral call on every member of his congregation?

Not necessarily. If the congregation is small, he probably

will want to for his own sake, if not for theirs. Even in some large churches, ministers find that a few months set aside at the outset of their ministry to get into every home gets them off to a good start. However, times are changing, and few things about the ministry have changed more markedly than the notion that a minister must keep going the rounds of his members, visiting regularly in the home of each. Some ministers confine their calling to the sick and prospects for membership. Some confine it entirely to the sick, and arrange for membership prospects to come to the church office to see them. Where there is a multiple staff, the entire visiting responsibility may rest with one man who was brought to the church to do this specific job. When I asked the minister of one of the largest Protestant churches in America how he determined what pastoral calls he would make, he said simply, "I call on my friends, as any other human being would do."

Various substitutes for calling have been devised. In many churches the parish plan has been developed so that the church may keep in closer touch with its people. Laymen are often organized to do extensive calling. The telephone is employed increasingly as a means of making a friendly visit in a matter of minutes. And much emphasis is being placed on the importance of organizing small face-to-face groups within the church membership. In addition to these ideas some ministers and their wives hold a series of teas or open-house events at their home. Over a period of time every church member receives an invitation to one of these. Once the membership has been covered, the parsonage family can keep up with the program by inviting each new membership class for an afternoon or evening in their home. Many ministers find they can have a meaningful relationship with more people by inviting groups to their home than by trying to get into the homes of all the people.

An additional word needs to be said about this because so many of the minister's guilt feelings center on this matter.

Many laymen, especially if they have been reared in a small rural church, expect their minister to call in their home and feel a very special kind of neglect if he never appears. Also some church officials who haven't kept up with current trends, and don't really know all that a minister has to do, continue to counsel the men to call from door to door. When the minister just can't find time to call on those people who have wondered why the minister never comes, and when his efforts to call geographically or alphabetically on all of his members have bogged down, he quickly becomes guilt-laden and defensive.

He shouldn't feel that way. Let him develop his own ministry and inform his people of what he is doing. Let him keep faithfully at his job, and not worry overmuch if he fails to do what someone else thought he should.

6. Should a minister take his wife along when he calls on single women, widows, or women whose husbands are away?

The answer to this is to use his common sense. Certainly he should avoid being in a home or even in the church alone with anyone of unsavory reputation, or anyone with whom an incident or rumors of an incident might develop. Both his wife and his secretary can be of great help to him in this regard.

7. What is the proper procedure for a minister to follow when he is approached concerning the possibility of accepting a call to another church?

The proper thing varies somewhat with the denomination. In some communions, for example, candidating for a pulpit is accepted procedure, while in others it is not in order. The first thing a man should do is to find out what the accepted procedure is in his denomination, and then adhere strictly to the rules of the game. Certainly no man is justified in expressing an interest in going to a church whose minister has not yet resigned or been appointed to another charge. There are official channels through which these things are handled, and they should be respected.

However, a good deal of initiative must rest with the minister himself. It is possible for him to do what seems to be the correct thing, and still get fouled up. In general, it is safe to say that concerned parties should be brought into the minister's confidence as early as possible. If a church approaches him, and he is at all interested, he should notify his denominational executive at once, and seek his counsel. If it looks as if he is going to want to accept the invitation, his own pulpit or pastoral relations committee should be consulted. They may have some things to say about the situation that would bear upon his decision. Besides they may be needlessly hurt if the minister's transfer comes as a total surprise. They might not have said or done a thing to discourage his move, but they like to feel they had a chance to if they so desired.

8. Is it necessary that a minister greet his people at the door following the service?

Not at all. This is a custom widely followed, and it provides a fine opportunity for the minister to have at least a casual contact with the people who are worshiping with him. Besides, the nice things people say as they file past him can set him up for the week! But many men make adaptations of this plan. Few, to be sure, slip out after a service without giving anyone a chance to greet them, but some prefer to remain at the chancel. This makes them available to any who wish to see them, but takes them out of the main line of traffic. That way those who don't care to speak to the minister may escape if they want to. Another fine plan is for the minister to go to a parlor or other suitable room following the service. The informal atmosphere makes for more relaxed conversation, and he has a chance to talk a little longer with some people who would have only a fleeting handshake if they met him at the door.

9. Is it proper to marry divorced persons?

For the answer to this, a man should consult his own conscience and the laws of his own denomination.

10. What constitutes proper dress for the minister?

This varies with the section of the country and the church. Where clerical garb is prescribed by the denomination, that's it. For others the rule is simply to follow what would be good taste for any gentleman. In some sections of the country there is a strong move toward greater informality. It is by no means necessary that a minister should always appear in dark clothing. Sometimes even sport jackets and slacks are in order. Certainly a minister should be clean. His trousers should be pressed and his shoes shined. However, in some rural or low-income areas, exaggerated attention to these matters could work against the minister and set him too much apart from his people.

Dark suits and black shoes are proper in the pulpit whether or not one wears a gown or pulpit robe. Simplicity is the thing here. There can be some color in ties and socks (though not in shirts), but the colors should be in keeping with the sanctuary and the service. Ecclesiastical vestments appropriate in one's denomination are always in order.

11. What constitutes plagiarism?

Recently one of my sons, who currently plans to be a preacher like his father, said, "Dad, when I get to be a preacher, I'll have to steal some of your sermons." When I asked what he meant by that, he expressed the fear that he would never be able to "think up" a sermon a week all by himself. I assured him that he was a little young to be worried about this, and that time would take care of his problem. After he finished high school, college, and seminary, I explained, he would understand better what goes into the making of a sermon, and he would have some resources to draw from.

I'm sure my son never heard of the word plagiarism, but he knows what stealing is, and at an early age he was aware of the fact that when he grew older he would be tempted to steal someone else's material.

Rare indeed is the man who is not aware of the temptation. Finding in a book something that is infinitely better than anything he could produce, he is tempted to put it into a sermon and pass it off as his own. Sometimes he does exactly that. And sometimes he modifies it just enough to mar the original artistry and make it sound more like something that might have come from his own pen. Feeling, as my son did, that he is unable to think up a sermon, he surrenders to the temptation to steal one.

Most seminary professors are aware of this tendency of men to plagiarize, and they preach against it. They challenge the students to be original and scold them severely for borrowing too much from the other fellow. Ministerial codes also carry firm words on the subject. One says, "It is unethical for the minister to use sermon material prepared by another without acknowledging the source from which it comes." And another says simply, "I will not plagiarize."

Some people feel the subject has been stressed too much. A psychologist told me recently that in her opinion ministers have been made to feel unnecessarily guilty about the matter. Conscientious ministers become worried for fear they are being dishonest even when their use of other material is well within proper bounds.

Part of the problem is that they don't know exactly what plagiarism is. And they aren't helped much by the advice I heard in my seminary days. We were told that a good test of whether or not material was being properly used was in answer to the question "Would I be embarrassed if the man who originally wrote it were in the congregation?" The only trouble with that is that some men would and some wouldn't. Some would be embarrassed when they shouldn't be, and some wouldn't be embarrassed when they should. A more dependable guide is needed.

Putting it simply, proper credit should always be given for quoted material. However, even original material usually has its source in something one has read or heard. The thing that makes it original is that it has passed through his mind, where it has been reshaped, mingled with different elements, and altered in its emphasis.

The problem with most men who are truly tempted to plagiarize is one of study habits. They have never learned to outline and prepare a sermon, and they tend to set aside too little time to do the job. The temptation to take a smooth paragraph from one of Fosdick's sermons is usually greatest on Saturday night. As has been emphasized earlier in this volume, creativity takes time. It is surprising how quickly one can free himself from the temptation to use someone else's material if he isn't working against the clock.

12. Is it proper for a minister or his wife to accept additional remunerative work to supplement their income?

Normally this is not wise, but there are circumstances when it is necessary. Before accepting such employment, however, a man should check carefully with the denominational executive most directly responsible for his work, and with the appropriate board in his church.

13. Should a minister and his wife consider it their social obligation to invite to dinner all persons who have entertained them in their homes?

The minister and his wife are in a rather unique position in this regard. Many people want to include them in dinner parties or other affairs they are having just because they want their pastor and his wife present. Normally it is a good idea for them to accept as many of these invitations as possible. It is a fine chance to get to know the people better. But there should be no sense of obligation to reciprocate with a similar invitation. Similarly, they should have no qualms of conscience about accepting gifts (unless, of course, they are too frequent or too extravagant, in which case they may be symptomatic of a psychological problem that needs attention) without giving equivalent ones in return. Church people want to do nice things for their pastor and his family in appreciation for the services they regularly render. This is a lovely tradition in the relationship between a minister and his people and should not be discouraged by putting it on a gift-for-gift, dinner-for-dinner basis. Along this same line, many churches make it a standing practice never to charge the minister and his wife for church dinners or other affairs where admission is by ticket or a stated price. They are always, and in a very special way, guests.

This is a grand thing for them to do, and the minister and his wife should never forget how privileged they really are. And they should take every precaution to see that their children do not grow up expecting special favors. On the receiving end of numerous courtesies, there is a grave danger that they will become presumptuous, accepting courtesies without ever extending so much as a note of thanks. This is difficult to excuse.

14. Should the minister and his wife give gifts to couples the minister marries?

If they are special friends, yes. If they were strangers until they came to get married, no. An exception, of course, is when a minister or his church makes it a practice to give a marriage booklet, a souvenir plate with a picture of the church, or some other suitable gift to every couple. This can get to be a financial burden on the minister himself if he has many weddings, but it is a nice thing for the church to do.

With most ministers, however, the problem has to do with couples in the church. If the responsibility does not become burdensome because of sheer numbers, a gift from the minister and his wife can be very meaningful to these young people. It is wise to give the same gift to all young couples. Some ministers select a suitable book. Others give every church couple they marry a Bible or a subscription to *The Christian Home*, or other similar magazine.

So much for the tensions that gather around the problem of what to do and when to do it. Only a few of the more common questions have been touched on here. The reader will think of additional ones. They might make interesting subjects for discussion for a group of neighboring ministers, a man and his wife, or a minister and his laymen.

XI

OUR FINAL LOYALTY

❖ ❖ ❖

People don't put the question so frequently any more, but it used to be common to ask a child, "Whose little boy are you?" This was the cue for the youngster to stick out his chest and affirm his paternity.

It is with that question that we come to the concluding chapter of this book. Not only the small child but the mature preacher needs to know the answer to the query, "And whose little boy are you?" To whom are you responsible?

The central problem of existence is the question of who is boss. Illustrations of this truth are all about us. The hive has its queen bee. A flock of geese requires a leader. The rooster rules the henyard.

On the human level, no one can be in uniform for long without developing a sharp eye for distinguishing rank; it is clearly defined to whom he gives orders and from whom he receives them. The totalitarian state has no difficulty in telling you whose orders no man questions; organized religion has its revered authorities; and those of us who are accustomed to democratic procedures are not comfortable until the election has been held and we have established who the top man is.

Unfortunately, however, the problem of who is boss is seldom solved by a neatly ordered hierarchy, whether the line of command is determined by a dictator's orders, democratic vote, or ecclesiastical seniority. Always we have those who rise up to question the leader: "What right does he have to give me orders?" they ask. Or, as the men of Jesus's time put it, "By what authority" does this man do these things? When Daniel was ordered to stop his praying, he refused to obey. Martin Luther defied the dictates of the Pope. Martin Niemoeller challenged Hitler. And the fully ordained associate is not always sure why he should take orders from the senior pastor. Who has the right to be boss?

This is the question that Jesus was struggling with in the Garden of Gethsemane. Over what did he have authority? Whom was he bound to obey? He entered the garden with his followers, and when he spoke they responded. He was their leader. "Sit here," he said, and they sat. "Remain here and watch with me," he ordered. "Watch and pray," he directed. "Rise, let us be going," he commanded. "Put your sword back in its place," he said. Yet when the soldiers came to take him, he submitted to their commands and went where he was ordered. But the real focus of the problem of who was boss in his life is seen in his prayer. "Let this cup pass from me," he cried; he was calling the play. "Not my will but thine be done," he concluded; he was bowing to a higher authority.

This is the struggle every minister must face. As he goes about his daily work, whose will is done? Some men are slaves to their wives who rule them with subtle but unyielding authority; some women are hemmed in by the dictates of a demanding husband. Children are often tyrannized by strict parents, and some parents surrender their own individuality to the undisciplined whims of their children. There are those whose actions are determined by their personal ambition, or by their fears. Others are directed by a spirit of love. Who is in charge in your life? Who calls the plays? You? Your enemies? Your friends? Your church board? Confusion? God?

In the struggle to determine the answer to this question, many people tie up with nervous tensions. Resentments build up when they follow the dictates of an authority they do not inwardly accept. Guilt poisons them when they listen to commands they know to be inferior but whose demands they cannot shake. Some come through the struggle by taking too much in their own hands; some become too submissive and lose their own will; some are thoroughly frustrated, never certain when to take charge and when to stand back.

It is a problem. Ministers, like other men, want to feel they are masterful. They pride themselves in being the pastor "in charge." Yet even the strongest leader gets his orders somewhere, whether he recognizes it or not. So the crucial question for each preacher is the question of his strongest loyalty. In the last analysis, whose little boy is he?

Success in the ministry depends on finding the right answer to that question. And the answer isn't altogether simple. A man must not only make up his mind whose son he *is* but also whose son he *isn't*. You see, he is often called on to play a role other than that of the little boy. As a matter of fact he has three distinct roles: son, brother, father. There are times when he must play the role of the child and take orders; there are times when he must play the role of the brother, neither giving orders nor submitting to them; and there are times when he must play the role of the parent, the man who is in command. The secret to a creative ministry is in learning what circumstances call for each role.

Taking them in reverse order, we begin with the minister as father. In spite of the practice, in some churches, of calling the minister Father Jones (although Jones perhaps doesn't seem like a sufficiently sanctified name), this should not characterize a minister's relationship with his parishioners. He is doing his people a distinct disservice if he fosters immaturity in them by encouraging them to think of him in the parent role. And he is fostering something worse than immaturity in himself. Occasionally in his congregation there will be youngsters whom some widow is heroically raising. If he can substitute as a father for them, he is rendering a needed service. But if he goes beyond this and encourages others to feel too dependent upon him, he is distinctly out of bounds. He is only feeding his own ego and stunting the spiritual growth of his people. The minister has no business being to his congregation what Jesus rejected being to his disciples. Jesus taught His followers to look not *to* Him, but *beyond* Him for their Father.

For the most part, the minister's role as father should be confined to nonpersonal reality: things, programs, ideas. A sermon is his brain child. He is both father and mother to it. He conceives it, and through great labor brings it to birth. It has his affection in a deeper sense than most people know. He has nurtured it and sacrificed for it, and finally sends it into the world with the prayer that it is mature enough to stand on its own feet. Occasionally a sermon is stillborn. This grieves him. Now and then he falls into sin and gives birth to a sermon that is not his own. Such illegitimate sermons are an embarrassment to him. He hopes their true paternity may not be discovered, and he feels guilty. But each year, when he is at his best he brings forth a family of healthy sermons. Some are brilliant; some are "plodders"; some are witty; some are just comfortable to be around. But he has fathered all of them and he has a right to claim them as his children.

He may also father creative programs. Sometimes he is only the stepfather to a litter he has taken over from someone else. And he may do a good job of nurturing them until they have reached their maturity. But he will find special satisfaction in guiding the growth of plans that he has been instrumental in forming. As "head of the house" his managerial skills will have a chance to develop. Like all good parents he will become an administrator.

Now it is important for the minister to take his father role seriously, for each of us requires for personal fulfillment the experience of being the boss, controlling something, being in command. A healthy person recognizes the areas in which he is in charge and assumes his leadership confidently. Every normal minister has the urge to direct things, and every church has plenty of things to be directed. But let the minister make sure it is *things* he is directing and not persons. Our paternal, managerial role is for nonpersonal reality. Elton and Pauline Trueblood had the right idea in their book, *The Recovery of Family Life*. They commented, "Housework must have been designed by God to keep a woman busy so that she would be at home, but too occupied to control the lives of the members of her family overmuch." The aggressive person who is not kept busy enough with nonpersonal reality—things, ideas, talents—sooner or later tries to control the lives of the people around him—his children, the members of his church, or whoever has the misfortune of crossing his path. Ministers who have slipped into this trap have carried their organizing ability too far.

It must be mentioned, however, that some men go to the opposite extreme. Instead of becoming controllers of the nonpersonal elements in their world, they have become slaves to them. They are subservient to a program or a building or a mimeograph machine. It is possible for a man to allow these things to govern his moods, determine his schedule, condition his convictions, and capture his spirit.

It is well known that some women are slaves to the house they live in. They haven't time to sit down with a child and read a book because the house needs cleaning. They can't turn aside for quiet meditation or a relaxed morning of reading because there are toys to pick up and a yard to clean. They can't stop to get directions from God because they are too busy getting their directions from their house, whose unwashed windows and dusty floors outshout the Almighty.

Many ministers fall into the same pit. The paraphernalia surrounding them dominates them. Called to be servants of God, they follow the commands of senseless automata. Perhaps this is what Paul referred to as being "carnally minded." Let no man succumb to this. Rather, when it comes to the nonpersonal elements in his ministry, let him stand to his full height and take charge.

A totally different attitude, however, is required in his relations with people. Here he should play the role of brother. To be a real person he needs to be able to say of others, "These are my kind. They are like me." It is important for children to have brothers and sisters, or at least playmates, so they can learn to build stable relations with others like themselves. No youngster develops normally if all his associations are with older persons who have authority over him. All of us must know a relationship in which there is mutuality, where those working with us are not our inferiors or our superiors but our associates, our peers.

And in Protestant Christianity this means all people: parishioners and ecclesiastical superiors, humble workmen and learned scholars. To bow to other humans as we would to God is degrading. In the days when Hitler was rising to power, a young Nazi said of his leader, "Whatever he commands, I will do." The folly of such devotion is evident. Not just because Hitler was a rascal, but because he was less than God, that man should have stopped short of surrendering his soul to him. Even if Hitler had been as saintly a man as Albert Schweitzer, he would have had no business requiring unlimited obedience to his commands. It is sacrilege to follow any man with a devotion that belongs only to God. "It is better to take refuge in the Lord," says the Psalmist, "than to put confidence in princes."

Bishop Kennedy once spent a leisurely evening with a man who had come to play an important role in government and had grown accustomed to rubbing elbows with famous people whose names are known in every household in America. "The most disillusioning thing about them," he said, "is to discover that they are not much smarter than I am." Noted leaders have their prejudices, their blind spots, their fits of indigestion, and their feelings of guilt just like the rest of us. They are our brothers, not our masters.

Hero worship is something that should be confined to adolescence. When we are adults we should know enough about human frailty not to think too highly of any man. It isn't that we become cynical, or are bent on debunking the saint. It is just that we have learned that perfection is to be found beyond the human sphere. We save ourselves a lot of disillusionment when we accept the fact that our favorite hero is a common sinner. On that day our relationship with him is strengthened because it is based on reality, and we love him for his humanness. He is our brother. It will be a healthy day for the Roman Catholic Church when it can see that the office of the Pope is subject to error, just as it was good for Japan to learn that the Emperor was not God. The democratic concept that "All men are created equal" leaves little room either for civil or ecclesiastical royalty. It is not good for human beings to bow to their fellows.

But it must also be said that it is not good for us to assume an air of superiority and be condescending toward others. Charles R. Brown was getting at this in his famous sermon on the text "Am I my brother's keeper?" He arrived at the conclusion that the answer is "No!" I am not my brother's keeper; I am my brother's brother and that is a very different matter.

Whenever we have one group of people assuming a paternalistic attitude toward another group of people, we are in for trouble. This is one of the most difficult problems on the international front today. How can we give the underdeveloped countries the assistance they need without insulting them, or jeopardizing their sense of dignity? When someone in the Great Decisions program asked of the people of other lands, "Why do they hate us when we have given them so much money?" the very question contained its answer. It is degrading to people to feel they are the objects of charity, even though they need the help, and the natural reaction is to hate the people who are in a position to be generous when they would like so much to be in that position themselves.

It is unwholesome for anyone to seek to exercise authority over the lives of others. No church is healthy when it is tyrannized by either laymen or ministers who insist that their word is law. Because the minister is the "head of the institution," he is faced with great temptations to treat people as things, and manipulate them. But to yield to the temptation is to surrender his qualification for being a leader.

In her autobiography, Marian Anderson tells of one woman who sought to play this kind of role. One day Miss Anderson arrived in a southern city where she was scheduled for a concert, and was met at the station by the woman who was concert manager. She addressed the famous contralto as "Marian," refusing to show a Negro the dignity of being addressed as "Miss Anderson." At the rehearsal the next afternoon, Miss Anderson found her accompanist and personal manager very angry about something, but they didn't seem disposed to tell her what it was, so she was content to let them keep it to themselves. She sang that night to a full house, an enthusiastic audience of 1,500 people. As was her custom, following certain numbers, she took the hand of her accompanist, a white man, as they stepped forward to take their bows together. The first time she did this, there was a momentary pause followed by a thunderous ovation. Each time the audience responded with enthusiastic applause.

Later that evening, as the artist and her accompanist and manager were on the train, the two men told her what had so upset them earlier in the afternoon. The woman who was the local concert manager had come to the rehearsal before Marian Anderson arrived and had asked, "Where is she?" "Do you mean Miss Anderson?" one of the men asked. Ignoring the question, she continued, "I understand that she goes out on the stage holding her accompanist's hand, and we won't stand for that here."

The other man said, "Miss Anderson would not think of coming here and telling you how to run your business. She has been on the stage long enough to know how to take care of her own business."

Commenting on that situation, Marian Anderson said, "I never sang in that town again, and it may not make any difference. But there were fifteen hundred people in that hall for whom one person was making a decision, and they had shown that they could make their own. It struck me that this one woman was assuming a heavy responsibility in thinking that she could decide for them."[1]

And ministers are assuming a heavy responsibility when they make arbitrary decisions for the parishioners as though they were dealing with children, incapable of ordering their own affairs. If we are to find real satisfaction in the ministry, we must learn to see all other humans as our brothers, refusing either to bow to them or to order their lives according to our liking. There is nothing quite so unbecoming a minister as failure to trust the basic good will and maturity of his people.

We come now to the obvious but often neglected truth that, in relation to God, the minister should play the role of the child. There is that within each of us which demands the experience of sonship if we are to be happy. We must bow to something; we must have an authority; there must be an ideal to look up to, a commander to listen to. Without this experience, something in us remains unfulfilled and we feel disinherited.

Think of the most dominant personality you know: the woman who is accusative, demanding, arbitrary—the man who gives definite orders and accepts no excuses when they are not followed. Are they happy people? No one who gives orders but never takes them can be happy, for we humans were not made to function that way. Youth who roam the streets at will, having shaken off parental restraints, free from anyone's dictates, are not happy youth. Even small children become disagreeable when they have succeeded in having the home organized to meet their demands. They need to know there is someone in charge of them.

Adults have the same need. The insecurities of life are such that they are ill at ease without the assurance that someone has things under control. So they look for a "parent." With some people a husband or wife plays the role. Many people look to their doctor as a parent. An authoritarian church substitutes for a dominant father in the lives of many. And often some other organization, a lodge or labor union, becomes the dominant influence in a person's life. The totalitarian state is papa for most of its subjects. John Gunther points out in his *Inside Russia Today* that "vast numbers of Russians now in responsible positions were sons and daughters of illiterate peasants, and have come up from nothing. . . . But they do not, as young people in America might, think of themselves as 'self-made'; they think of themselves as *state*-made."

Of course none of these parent substitutes are adequate. An adult who leans, childlike, on another person, church, or government is allowing himself to be too dependent and permitting someone else to have too much authority. Nevertheless, everyone must have someone or something he looks up to. In the last analysis he is not the captain of his soul nor the master of his fate. He is a created being, dependent for his very existence upon some power beyond himself. Most churches no longer require a bride to promise to "obey" her husband. But this does not release her from the need to obey somebody. We are grateful that those words have been taken from the wedding ceremony, but whoever put them in at least understood that when a girl leaves the home of her parents she is not free. She is still responsible to someone. What they didn't realize is that the young husband is not the one she is responsible to. He needs someone to obey as much as she.

Jesus was aware of this. A master psychologist and spiritual genius, He understood man's need for guidance, love, discipline, and all those elements we associate with parenthood. So he directs us to God as *Father!* When we have attained a degree of maturity as persons and as ministers, then it is God's orders we follow; it is His will we seek to do. When we carry on the arduous and demanding work of our calling, it is He whom we serve. It is important for the minister to remember that when he visits a cantankerous member, calls at the hospital, takes a load of youngsters to a convention, or burns the midnight oil to complete a sermon, he is not a spineless creature being pushed and hauled hither and yon by the erratic demands of his parishioners. He is serving God!

We are sometimes prone to forget this. We accept a pastorate and call it ours. We set up committees and run them to suit ourselves. We develop a program, assuming we can handle it the way we choose. But that's all wrong. Our churches aren't ours; our committees don't belong to us; our programs are not our personal genius come to flower. All are God's and we handle that which is God's aright only as we follow orders that originate with Him, and not with ourselves.

And we get our orders through prayer. No one would have much respect for a minister who wasn't a praying man. Although many laymen do not pray, except in emergencies, it gives them a good deal of satisfaction to know their preacher prays. And of course he does—at least in the Sunday-morning service and when called on to open a meeting "with a word of prayer." Few ministers, however, have a well-developed devotional life. So far most laymen don't know this, and the ministers don't go out of their way to inform them. But this is the Achilles heel of many a popular preacher. He is banking on his own charm and native ability and neglecting the upper room.

One day a spiritually disturbed man came in to see me. He had found life frightening and confusing, and someone had told him I might help him get things straightened out. He had taken a drink or two before he came, possibly to get up his courage. Two things dominated his thinking: war and God. He was a soldier and twice had experienced war first hand; once in World War II, and once in the Korean conflict. It had sickened him. But he wasn't sure he had ever experienced God at all. "I want to find God," he said. "I've been looking for a long time. It seems like I've been looking a hundred years." Then the shadows in his face deepened as he related, "I put a bayonet through a fellow once—up against a palm tree—and I got to thinking afterward, maybe I put the dog-gone bayonet through God."

I don't know how many people have bayoneted God. It must have been something like that which happened one afternoon on a hill on the outskirts of Jerusalem. But many of us are inclined to ignore Him. And that's just as bad—possibly worse.

The truth is that what we ministers need more than anything else is the same thing our laymen need: renewed awareness of God as our Father; reassurance that He loves us. In the last analysis, most of us, in spite of the praise we get and the self-confidence we so often appear to have, are timid and unsure of ourselves. We come to our churches a little like the country boy going to his first party—not quite sure why we were invited. Involved in the work of the church, we sometimes find it hard to love others, but at that we often find it easier to love them than to believe others love us. Most of all, it is quite frankly difficult to believe that God loves us.

But this is the message Jesus taught; it is the message we preach, and it must also be the message we *believe*. In a single sentence in the Gospel of John, Jesus presents this wonderful truth simply and forcefully: "God so loved the world that he gave his only Son." Repeatedly He emphasized the basic idea that the God who created all things has placed a high value on persons. "Look at the birds of the air"; he said, "they neither sow nor reap nor gather into barns, and yet your heavenly Father feeds them. Are you not of more value than they? . . . Consider the lilies of the field, how they grow; they neither toil nor spin; yet I tell you, even Solomon in all his glory was not arrayed like one of these. But if God so clothes the grass of the field, which today is alive and tomorrow is thrown into the oven, will he not much more clothe you?" He used many illustrations to get this basic idea over. "Are not two sparrows sold for a penny?" he asked one day. "And not one of them will fall to the ground without your Father's will. . . . Fear not, therefore; you are of more value than many sparrows." On another occasion, he compared God with a father, saying, "What man of you, if his son asks him for a loaf, will give him a stone? Or if he asks for a fish, will give him a serpent? If you then, who are evil, know how to give good gifts to your children, how much more will your Father who is in heaven give good things to those who ask him?" These are only a few of the illustrations He used. Through the parables of the Lost Sheep, and the Lost Coin, and the Prodigal Son, and in many other ways, He emphasized and re-emphasized this central idea: God loves us.

I suspect that Jesus said so much about this because it is so hard for people to accept. It is difficult for us to believe that anyone who amounts to anything could really think highly of us. Knowing my own shortcomings as I do, I find it hard to know how my wife and children can love me with any consistency, and I am always surprised when anyone whom I admire expresses affection or appreciation for me. This I think is a human characteristic, and it is the reason that lovers ask each other to repeat again and again the simple formula: "I love you." They find it hard to believe it's true, so demand continual reassurance and demonstration.

Perhaps the most poignant experience of the human spirit

is right here: the fear that one is not held to be of value, that he would be easily overlooked, or forgotten. The touching cry of the thief on the cross expresses this feeling: "Jesus remember me when you come in your kingly power." He voices the cry of all men—tell me you love me, that I'm not worthless, that I'm worth saving.

Realizing how deep in human nature is the fear that one does not ultimately count, that he may in the long run be punished, or worse, disregarded by the Creator, you can understand why the message Jesus brought was considered to be *Good News*. And it is good news for the pulpit as well as for the pew. We need not look elsewhere for parent substitutes. We have a Father who loves us, in whom "we live and move and have our being."

If we are caught up in the spirit of this, the heavy load of our vocation will seem lighter. There will be much to do, and we will finally burn ourselves out doing it, but there will be joy in the burning. Ours will be the spirit of the little old lady in the Montgomery bus strike. After she had been walking for several weeks, someone asked if she were tired. She answered, "My feet is tired, but my soul is at rest."

Well, whose little boy are you? That is the question every minister must answer for himself. He must determine with care to whom he gives orders, with whom he lives on a level of equality, and from whom he takes orders. In the last analysis, the job of the Christian minister is this: *in cooperation with his brother man, to become a responsible administrator of the work God wants him to do.*

When he functions in this manner, he will not be free from all tensions. That will never happen, and never should happen in this life. But he will have learned to use his tensions as an archer uses his taut bow to send his arrow to its mark. Perhaps that is what Paul was talking about when he wrote to the people in the church at Corinth, stating that he did not wish "to bring discredit on the ministry God has given us." Continuing, he said,

Indeed we want to prove ourselves genuine ministers of God whatever we have to go through—patient endurance of troubles or even disasters, being flogged or imprisoned; being mobbed, having to work like slaves, having to go without food or sleep. All this we want to meet with sincerity, insight and patience; with genuine love, speaking the plain truth, and living by the power of God. Our sole defence, our only weapon, is a life of integrity, whether we meet honour or dishonour, praise or blame. Called "impostors" we must be true, called "nobodies" we must be in the public eye. Never far from death, yet here we are alive, always "going through it" yet never "going under." We know sorrow, yet our joy is inextinguishable. We have "nothing to bless ourselves with" yet we bless many others with true riches. We are penniless, and yet in reality we have everything worth having (Phillips).

NOTES

I. CONDEMNED TO SIN PIOUSLY

1. John Baillie, *A Diary of Private Prayer* (New York, Charles Scribner's Sons, 1949), p. 15.
2. Harold B. Walker, *Power to Manage Yourself* (New York, Harper & Brothers, 1955), p. 18.
3. Jeanne D'Orge, in *The New York Times Book Review*.

II. THE STRUGGLE TO LOVE OUR ENEMIES

1. Pierre van Paasen, *Days of Our Years* (Hillman-Curl, Inc., 1939), p. 241.
2. Richard Gehman, *A Murder in Paradise* (New York, Rinehart & Company, 1954), p. 94.
3. André Maurois, *Disraeli* (New York, D. Appleton & Company, 1928), p. 104.
4. Hanns Lilje, *The Valley of The Shadow* (Philadelphia, Muhlenberg Press, n.d.), p. 40.
5. Martin Luther King, Jr., *Stride Toward Freedom* (New York, Harper & Brothers, 1958), p. 103.

III. COMPETING WITH OUR BROTHERS

1. Gerald Kennedy, *I Believe* (New York, Abingdon Press, 1958), p. 24.
2. Harold B. Walker, *Power to Manage Yourself* (New York, Harper & Brothers, 1955), p. 18.

V. SPIRITUAL PREACHING AND MATERIAL COMFORT

1. James H. Robinson, *Adventurous Preaching* (Great Neck, N.Y., Channel Press, 1956), p. 157.
2. Robert M. Bartlett, *They Dared to Live* (New York, Association Press, 1937), p. 29.
3. Harry Emerson Fosdick, *The Living of These Days* (New York, Harper & Brothers, 1956), p. 193.
4. Ralph Stoody, "Service Is The Secret," in *The New Christian Advocate*, January, 1958, p. 41.

VI. THE PROFESSIONAL FAMILY MAN

1. William H. Whyte, Jr., *The Organization Man* (Garden City, N.Y., Doubleday Anchor Books, Doubleday & Company, Inc., 1957), p. 162.
2. *Ibid.*, pp. 157–158.

3. Elton and Pauline Trueblood, *The Recovery of Family Life* (New York, Harper & Brothers, 1953), p. 79.

4. Gerald Kennedy, *The Christian and His America* (New York, Harper & Brothers, 1958), p. 136.

5. Martin Luther King, Jr., *Stride Toward Freedom* (New York, Harper & Brothers, 1958), pp. 123–124.

VII. DISCIPLINED DISORDER

1. John Henry Jowett, *The Preacher: His Life and Work* (New York, Abingdon Press, (1912), p. 116.

2. Thomas F. Chilcote, Jr., *The Excellence Of Our Calling, An Abridgment of Phillips Brooks' Lectures on Preaching* (New York, E. P. Dutton & Company, Inc., 1954), p. 55.

3. Rudolf Flesch, *The Art of Clear Thinking* (New York, Harper & Brothers, 1951), p. 146.

4. *Ibid.*, p. 147.

VIII. DENOMINATIONALLY ECUMENICAL

1. F. Gerald Ensley, "Methodism In The Ecumenical Movement," *The New Christian Advocate*, December, 1958, pp. 29–30.

IX. AFRAID TO BE RADICAL

1. *The Autobiography of Benjamin Franklin* (New York, Pocket Books, Inc.), p. 22.

2. William J. Lederer and Eugene Burdick, *The Ugly American* (New York, W. W. Norton & Company, Inc., 1958), p. 170.

3. Harry Emerson Fosdick, *The Living of These Days* (New York, Harper & Brothers, 1956), p. 157.

4. *The New Christian Advocate*, October, 1958, p. 52.

5. C. Wright Mills, *The Causes of World War Three* (New York, Simon and Schuster, 1958), pp. 146, 156.

X. THE RIGHT THING AT THE RIGHT TIME

1. Codes for the Congregational, Disciples, Methodist, Presbyterian, and Unitarian denominations may be found in the Appendix to Nolan B. Harmon's *Ministerial Ethics and Etiquette* (Nashville, Abingdon-Cokesbury Press, 1950).

XI. OUR FINAL LOYALTY

1. Marian Anderson, *My Lord, What a Morning* (New York, The Viking Press, 1956), p. 245.

INDEX

✤ ✤ ✤